THE SYLVAN PATH

ALSO BY GARY FERGUSON

Spirits of the Wild: The World's Great Nature Myths

The Yellowstone Wolves: The First Year

Walking Down the Wild

THE SYLVAN PATH

A Journey Through America's Forests

GARY FERGUSON

St. Martin's Press New York

A THOMAS DUNNE BOOK.
An imprint of St. Martin's Press

Design by Pei Loi Koay

Library of Congress Cataloging-in-Publication Data

Ferguson, Gary, 1956–
The sylvan path : a journey through America's forests / by Gary Ferguson.
p. cm.
"A Thomas Dunne book."
ISBN 0-312-15219-1
1. United States—Description and travel—Anecdotes. 2. Forest reserves—United States—Anecdotes. 3. Ferguson, Gary, 1956—Journeys—United States—Anecdotes. 4. National characteristics, American—anecdotes. I. Title.
E169.04.F467 1997
917.304'92—dc21 96-46058
CIP

First Edition: March 1997

10 9 8 7 6 5 4 3 2 1

for Pearl

Acknowledgments

My sincere thanks go to the splendid librarians and researchers at Yale University, Boston Public Library, Maine State Historical Collections, the University of Tennessee, Indiana University Folklore Collections, Northern Michigan University, and American Forests. Also to Bev Twillman, a wise and wonderful storyteller, and to the generous, caring directors of the Montana, East Tennessee, Minnesota, and Maine Community Foundations.

And last but by no means least, thanks to all the people of the woods. It's through their lives that I again found the joy of wild places.

THE SYLVAN PATH

Introduction

As near as I remember I left the ordinary when I was seven, in late summer, out with my parents off some potholed county road in northern Indiana on a hazy Sunday afternoon when the mayapples were hung and the milkweed was in full flower. My folks had packed lunch and driven my brother and me out some ten or fifteen miles from town, one thing in mind: to let us climb trees. There I was, standing in the crook of a maple, twelve feet off the ground, hugging the trunk, curtains of big green leaves wound up in the wind and dancing all over the place, making noises like a fast creek running through the sky. And my father, looking up at me from ground level through the scratched lenses of his gray-plastic glasses, muscled arms outstretched to catch me if I fell.

Thoughts of the woods have been with me ever since. They come in daydreams: sycamores and sugar maples with arms locked on the hilltops near Lake Wawasee; in the bottoms down below, crowds of pawpaw and white oak and hickory. They rise as pieces of past vacations spent rolling down some two-lane—first in a Studebaker, then in a Chevy—the back windows open, staring into timber: sprawls of tamarack and jack pine in Michigan, unbroken but for log taverns with halos of blue light from the Hamms beer signs in the tops of the windows. In Tennessee, dizzy rolls of red oak, chestnut, and shagbark hickory falling away from the top of the Cumberland Plateau.

We first went west in 1966, to Colorado, and I met the Rocky Mountains with my chin on the back of the seat, staring wide-eyed through the windshield. But there too it was the great sweeps of conifers—Douglas-fir, Englemann spruce, lodgepole pine—that lent mystery to the mountains, that brought a feeling of possibility to those drifts of stone. Even now, the lion's share of my childhood memories is shot full of leaves.

Which is why it was such a sad surprise when in my mid-thirties I looked over my shoulder to find that the trees had shrunk from my life, that they'd gone from being nothing short of ladders to the sky to being something merely pleasant; stories, where once there was myth. Of course fascinations don't really burn up in flash fires so much as they drown by degrees—old dreams like old boats, sopping water, growing heavier with every season, harder to steer. And yet if I had to pick the heart of those troubled times, it was probably when I went home to Indiana after my mother's death in 1988, hoping for one more ramble through some of the unkempt places I'd known as a child. But all I could see were the losses. Old wetlands, once thick with the smell of creation, shrouded in veils of pussy willow and spicebush, had been drained away, packed in dirt, filled with condominiums. Fence rows near Cromwell were plowed under, taking with them the fox and the raccoon, the songbirds that once hid in their thickets. Gone too the woodlots that had slept away the winters beside those yellow, stubbled fields of corn.

It was years later that I was wandering through the stacks of a library in Boulder, Colorado, when I stumbled across a passage about an all but forgotten American named Joe Knowles. On a rainy August day in 1913, this part-time artist, then in his mid-forties, stripped down to a G-string, shook hands with a group of bewildered reporters on the shore of King and Bartlett Lake in western Maine, then trudged off into the woods without a single piece of equipment to live as a wild man for sixty days. The idea, Knowles claimed, came from a dream in which he was lost in the woods, alone and naked, with little hope of getting out. "Not much of a dream," he confessed, "but a damn real one."

Joe Knowles emerged from the forest two months later a full-blown hero. Two hundred thousand people in Maine and Massachusetts turned out to see him—20,000 on the Boston Common alone. A book of his adventures sold more than 300,000 copies, and he toured vaudeville with top billing, preaching the virtues of life beyond the bustle and soot of the twentieth century. The next summer Knowles managed a similar feat—again to the cheers of the nation—this time in the Siskyou Mountains of southwest Oregon.

For whatever reason Joe chose to act out his "damn real dream," he tapped into a belief, once commonplace, whose time had come again. It said that if our dance with nature had been such a big part of what we most valued about our character, then losing our wild places might mean losing that which held the best hope for the future. It was like gas to a spark. The land-preservation movement exploded. Youth groups sprang up everywhere—the Sons of Daniel Boone, the Boy Pioneers, the Boy Scouts, the Woodcraft Indians—each dedicated to maintaining the influence of the wilderness in children's lives. In the years between 1910 and 1940, *The Boy Scout Handbook* outsold every book in America except the Bible. Frontier historian Frederick Jackson Turner—the guy who said that in America, democracy was a forest product—was suddenly a genius. The woods were alive again in the American psyche.

Most historians say that Joe Knowles was a charlatan, that he never really did what he claimed to have done. They may be right. Still, he was the one who reminded me that our willingness to conquer nature has as often as not been tethered to a longing to save it—that there have in fact been generous times, times when we've waltzed with the woods like Cinderella on champagne. While early Christians were full of fears about wild places, the sons and daughters who steered America through its formative years courted those places, seeding a national commons of fable and myth and spirit-tales based on mountains and rivers and forests.

As unlikely an inspiration as Joe Knowles might be, he's the one who left me hungry to go back out and roam the last wild places, places like Maine and Appalachia and the North Woods, looking for the people who still had pieces of the old American imagination in their pockets, people who never forgot how to warm their lives with the woods.

Chapter One

The morning sun is ripping holes in the fog, leaving scattered herds of gray ghosts running for cover in the grassy knolls off Frenchman Bay. Now and then one climbs the heights and glides across the campus, gives us a damp, chilling hug as it passes, then disappears into the quiet streets of Bar Harbor.

I'm on my knees again. The second day of it, hovering over a washtub filled with bundles of white-spruce roots. Simple work, really. Pluck a root out of the water, uncoil it, strip away the bark by pulling the length of it through a tight, narrow split in a wooden stake driven into the ground; then recoil it and place it into another tub of water. If the root's too thick—bigger, say, than a pencil—you cut it in half lengthwise with a utility knife. I'm still a little nervous about that part, worried that I'll slip and sever it, and the fact is, it takes a heck of a lot of effort to dig these things out of the ground. The tannin in the water has turned my fingers the color of copper, puckered my skin into the hands of an old man. But I've soaked up this wonderful scent, this smell like pepper and pine.

I remember sitting at home in Montana two weeks ago, thinking of how great it would be to start this summer of trees with some kind of ritual. Some occasion, a starting gun that years from now I could look back on and say it all began on this day or that, with those people, in the heat or the wind or the thunder. It dawns on me now that this is it.

My teacher is a Penobscot Indian named Barry Dana—a solid, good-looking man in his early thirties, tanned and fit, someone you'd expect to find modeling clothes for Land's End. But here he is on his knees working these enormous sheets of birch bark, using a bone awl from the shin of a moose to punch lines of vertical holes along the outer edges. Once that's done, he lays the sheets side by side, the edges slightly overlapped, and places a thin batten of mountain maple over the seam. Then come my white-spruce roots, which serve as thread for sewing the panels together, sheet after sheet, until they turn into dazzling runs of bark some twelve feet long. As each length is finished, I leave my root buckets, and Barry, his wife, Lori, and I maneuver the panels onto a squat, dome-shaped frame of white-ash poles, then make them fast with ties from the inner bark of basswood. A Penobscot wigwam. Since the outer surface of birch bark is more prone to weathering, the sheets are placed on the frame with the papery side facing in, which makes the inside room quiet and homey, a womb of oyster-white scored with thin black lines and blisters shaped like crescent moons. A fire at night dances on the walls, drawing them in and then releasing them. Rhythmic, like breathing.

Really I came here to the coast of Maine for just a brief visit—a little talk with Barry, maybe some lunch, but then he invited me to spend some time actually working on his wigwam, and that changed everything. There's something about the cadence of this shaping wood by hand, a patient, unhurried rhythm that over time leaves even quiet people like Barry suddenly generous with their thoughts. Yesterday we were stripping basswood bark for framing ties when he laid out this dream he has for a group of Penobscot teenagers. "Some summer," he says, "I'll take a bunch of kids and we'll build an entire village of these things." He tells it like it's fact. "We'll make birch canoes, too. Then we'll set out from that village on a long trip up some historic river trail. It'll be incredible." I keep thinking about those kids slipping into their canoes—canoes they released from trees. The startled look on their faces when they push on the paddles and the thing skitters forward like some kind of water strider, as if it were being pulled by an invisible hand.

Something else Barry talks about is his love for running. He says the Penobscots used to have an elite group of gifted running men who carried messages in times of war—men so fast and nimble they could run down deer in a thick woods. They enjoyed few of the common pleasures that other people took for granted. No sex, for one thing. Strictly controlled diets. Sleeping as a group in one big wigwam, an elder standing by with a switch in his hand, watching so each man kept his legs crooked to the proper position throughout the night. They called them the "Pure Men."

Every summer Barry makes a trek with some young Penobscots, running a hundred miles from Indian Island to the base of Maine's greatest peak, the old giant, Mount Katahdin. It occurs to me that in the difficult hours—those painful miles when you think you're going to either pass out or at the very least, throw up on your shoes—stories of the Pure Men must seem like extra breath.

All day long people on the street have been catching glimpses of the wigwam, this cinnamon-colored dome nestled in the cedars, and a lot of them have wheeled in for a closer look. Almost like they can't help it. "It's so beautiful," says a woman from Kansas City, maybe forty-five, while her husband circles it, pokes his head through the east-facing door. "Will you be staying in it tonight?" he wants to know.

"Not me," says Barry. "I've got a motel room with a shower and a TV."

Fifteen minutes later, Bev spots the wigwam from halfway across campus, clutches her books tight to her chest and runs over. "Oh wow," she says, panting hard to catch her breath. "I can't believe this. It's just the way I saw it. This is going to sound really strange, but . . . well, I'm studying to be a midwife. Last month I started dreaming about helping women give birth inside a wigwam. It looked just like this."

Barry nods, keeps quiet. She waits. "What do you think that means?" she finally asks.

He smiles, tells her it's not for him to decide. "Put it in your life where it fits best," he says.

To me, the dream seems perfect. Back in the 1920s, paper birch was chosen as America's "Mothers' Tree," which is why you can still find it growing at the White House, where it was planted to honor the mothers of the presidents; and at the Capitol, for the mothers of the nation; at Arlington National Cemetery, for the moms of fallen soldiers.

"Can I touch it?" Bev asks, looking hopeful. And she walks up and lays the flat of her hand against the skin of the inner bark, just like I've seen Barry do at the end of the day when we've finished working.

Around eleven we take a break, lie on the grass beside the wigwam, eat bagels and drink coffee and play with Barry and Lori's eleven-month-old daughter Sik^w ani—the Penobscot word for springtime. In the two days I've been here, Sik^w ani has never once strayed from these pieces of the forest. She snubs squeaky ducks and Fisher-Price blocks in favor of sheets of birch bark—hugs them, rubs her cheeks on them, smiles like a blue sky whenever she feels them against the bottoms of her bare feet. When she's not fondling birch she's chewing on spruce roots, or running her fingers through the ribbons of basswood bark, or wobbling over for another whiff from the bucket of sealing pitch. When she sits on my lap I can smell the forest in her hair.

Lori is saying that the best part of working with birch bark is going out and finding the trees. Being out in the woods in early spring looking for that special one—the way the trunk glows against the dark of the balsam and spruce. There's a strong smell of sap when the knife blade cuts through the outer layers of the bark. And then a loud "pop" as it releases from the tree.

We've set about our work again when a friend of Barry's shows up: a woman in her sixties, a Penobscot artist from North Branch who's come to town to be part of a weekend art show. She works with birch too, though her talent lies in using knives to make fine engravings on the inner bark, slicing delicate lines through the thin, rust-red winter layer to reveal the buff underneath. She describes her latest project to me—a series of three panels depicting her last deer hunt. She stays for a long time, just sitting quietly while we work—Lori scraping bark, Barry sewing, me with my roots.

Nearby, a class of fifth-graders is playing some kind of nature game where the kids are supposed to act like different parts and processes in the life of trees: leaves falling, random visits by woodpeckers and bees, rain being sucked up along the lateral roots, nuts falling, water pumping up the xylem, moisture rising to the clouds through transpiration.

"People are adrift these days," the Penobscot woman says to me out of the blue. "It's because they don't have acts of creation in their lives."

And that's all she cares to say about it. Later on, driving west across Maine in my van. I'll find it hard to get that comment out of my head. In the end I'll decide that people in America start out giving birth to all kinds of creative acts. But when those acts turn into something different than we imagined, something less than perfect, we walk away, tell ourselves it wasn't meant to be. One of the most comforting things about the old Penobscot world is that the creators made mistakes all the time.

The great giant Gluskap, who created humans by shooting arrows into the trees, splitting the trunks and allowing the first men and women to step out into the world, was just a guy of average intelligence, a kind of blue-collar superhuman who learned as he went. Take fish. When he first started making them he was all thumbs, which is why even today some, like puffers and toadfish, are so incredibly homely. Likewise, Gluskap's squirrels used to be enormous. Later on, when people stumbled onto the scene, Squirrel went berserk, running around gnawing off trees, tossing boulders around—a real loose cannon. Gluskap called him over and soothed his fever by petting him. Each time his hand stroked Squirrel's back, the creature got smaller and smaller (and its tail curled a little more), until it reached the size and shape we see today. Squirrel still runs around chattering and tossing nuts at the sight of people, but let's face it, the damage is trifling. Grasshoppers, skunks, moose, beaver—all of them were works in progress. Gluskap just kept fussing until he got it right.

It's nearly dark when we call it quits. All that's left to do is seal the seams with pitch, then secure the bark with an exterior frame of ash poles. I'm leaving tonight, heading west to chase the ghost of Joe Knowles, so I'll miss those final touches. Sik^{w} ani is asleep in the car seat, and Barry, Lori, and I sit on the grass in the last of the light, mostly just looking at the wigwam.

"If we were going to use it in really cold weather," Barry says, "we'd put another run of birch bark on the inside of the main frame, then stuff moss into the space between the layers. When you're ready to move—maybe it's time to go where the salmon are running—you just take off the panels, roll them up like a rug and be on your way. Use them on other frames in other places." Ingenious, really. It's curious that the earliest colonists, who were in no small measure ramblers themselves, used to sneer at the Penobscots for being so nomadic. Finally they claimed that the Indians' refusal to stay put and farm was a breaking of biblical law, a transgression that left them ineligible to own land.

We finish loading the last of the tools, say our good-byes, and just like that, they're driving off into the night toward Bar Harbor, the taillights of the minivan blurring in a thin sheet of fog. I walk over to the wigwam one last time, lay my hands against the cinnamon-colored bark, find myself hoping for an act of creation.

Chapter Two

Sometime in the tar black of last night Cirrus sneaked over the lip of the east horizon for the first time this year, and with a tiny blink of white light, ushered in the dog days of summer. It will be hot today. Over ninety. Grainy clouds of flies and mosquitoes are already pushing through the forest, driving moose onto roadways and into water up to their necks, setting the ears of whitetails to a crazy twitching, as if something was short-circuiting inside. At an old tie bridge I watch the Dead River ease south in the dawn light without a whisper; it gathers up the springs and creeks gently, the way a person collects blackberries at the end of the picking season, handling the overripe fruit with exaggerated care, trying hard not to bruise it.

Well beyond the banks of the Dead River, the terrain runs level for a while, bumps once or twice, then makes a sudden rise some thousand feet into crumpled loaves, leaving the horizon looking as though someone had slammed the oven door on a half-done soufflé. And yet the weight of the uplands can't erase the feeling that this is a subtle place, a place of nooks and crannies: small bowls scooped out of the pine-covered hills where black bears snooze in the afternoon heat; smooth blades of granite plunging into gardens of bracken fern; muddy passages cut by beaver into the grassy skin of the willow islands.

This is my second trip in as many days up this twisted gravel road to King and Bartlett Lake—point of departure in 1913 for wild man Joe Knowles. Yesterday everything ground to a halt some eight miles from the lake, at a roadblock made of steel cable hung with tattered ribbons of logging tape. And a plywood sign: "Private Camp–No Trespassing"—the hand-lettered words served up by someone either impatient or uninspired, slanted and uneven, trickles of paint hanging from the corners of the letters. From its anchor to a big pine, the cable crossed the road, then headed over open ground to the side of a small, slumped wooden cottage, passing into the front porch through a small box about the size of a telephone book. Behind the porch screen, a half-dozen people in fishing hats were slumped in lawn chairs, heads tilted back toward the ceiling, then rocking forward again, fastened to cans of beer.

"No sir," the lone woman on the porch tells me when I ask about going through, folding her ample arms, which are flushed and bitten by the out-of-doors. I scan the other faces—all belonging to men, mostly middle-aged and older—looking for encouragement. But they merely nod and stare at the floor. "Just can't let you through," the woman says. "The place is for registered guests only." Without thinking I ask whether it'd be okay to grab my backpack and walk in the eight miles from here. Beers stop in midair and faces turn, openmouthed, as if trying to figure out if I'm being funny, sarcastic, or just plain stupid.

And that was when I knew the only chance I had of making it to King and Bartlett short of an air drop was to ride in on Joe Knowles's coattails. So I squatted on my haunches beside the empties and the pretzel bowls and started recounting the strange story of this middle-aged wild man, buck-naked, disappearing into these same woods for two months just to prove that the average American still had sap in his veins. Thankfully, some of the older men have heard of Knowles — actually grew up with older relatives telling the tale. Maybe it's the beer, but for whatever reason they seem to turn wistful at the mere mention of it, eager to remember if not the story, then at least the tellings.

By the time I finish with Joe Knowles going off on a vaudeville tour, I've been offered a lawn chair and a cold can of Busch, and the woman is calling the owner of the camp to see if it's okay for me to come up and look around. On the phone, she's downright enthusiastic. "He's researching this wild-man thing," she says, then turns to me, passing on the owner's approval with a quick nod. When she hangs up we talk a little more. She tells me how the fishing's been slow, how the flies are so bad this year that moose are crazy with them, bolting onto highways and being killed by cars.

After ten or fifteen minutes, I finish off my beer, offer my thanks, tell them I hope the fish start coming around and head back to the van. As I pull forward, the cable drops onto the road, lowered from the porch by one of the men sitting within arm's reach of a trailer crank screwed into the small box the size of a telephone book on the side of the cottage wall.

I find Fred Thurston sitting in a room off the back side of the kitchen in an old lodge — a classic woodland building, comforting with its stone fireplace and heavy logs, its big stuffed furniture meant for big stuffed men. Thurston is a thick-legged, heavy-fingered, barrel-chested Welshman, sitting like a coach with his team of guides by his side, drinking fifty-dollar-a-bottle cabernet. His wife Betsy is there, too —

an attractive, poised, forty-something woman in khaki shorts and a safari blouse, busy spilling out details of her latest sail-fishing exploits in the Caribbean.

"Ah yeah," Fred says when I mention Knowles, nodding his head, seeming plenty familiar with the story. "Probably didn't really do all that, though. At least most of the old-timers around here don't think so. But then, what the hell do we know?"

For a long time Fred and Betsy Thurston were guests at the King and Bartlett Camp, coming year after year to unwind, using it as a combination spa, summer camp, and neighborhood tap. Finally they just up and bought the place, funding the purchase with part of a small fortune made juggling more fast-food chicken franchises than probably even the Colonel ever intended of one couple. Between stories of carousing in gambling houses in the Bahamas with a certain famous country-music star, Fred invites me to poke around for as long as I like—even offers me the services of his guides. The last of the wine disappears around midnight; Fred gets up, suggests I follow him and Betsy home, says I can use their house as a place to sleep and work. Back at the cable roadblock, Fred honks his horn and someone sitting in the dark on the porch of the cottage cranks down the wire and we go roaring off toward Eustis at fifty miles an hour in a cloud of dust. Rolling hell-bent through the woods, I'm thinking I really should've gotten around to putting those deer whistles somebody gave me three years ago on the front bumper of my van. Then I could be busy right now praying that they work for moose.

At around four in the morning, somewhere in the thick of a wine sleep, that country-music singer we were talking about earlier eases through the front door, accompanied by Fred's son and his girlfriend, creeps up the steps, throws open the door to the bedroom beside mine and with a blood-curdling holler that would scare the hell out of any audience at the Grand Ol' Opry, leaps into bed with Fred and Betsy.

Fred lets out a roar, shocked, like a snoozing bear being launched with a douse of ice water. That peters out into cursing, chiding. "You crazy little shit!" Pretty soon the whole troupe shuffles past my door and down the stairs into the kitchen. I lie in bed until about four-thirty, then head down to join them. Everyone is dressed, fresh cocktails in hand, talking about fishing. Fred smirks at me when I walk in. "Christ, he says. "You guys from Montana sure like to sleep late."

By the time I reach King and Bartlett this morning, an east wind is up. Six-inch waves are running arm in arm past the boats of the fishing camp, past the pontoons of the float plane, cresting at the beach in flashing lines that throw off the reds and silvers of the sunrise. The guides are huddled in the back room again, this time peering out the windows, fretting that their clients won't be able to fly-fish in such choppy water. "She'll lay down this afternoon," Glen says, turning away from the window to search for his mug of coffee. Two drakes roar over the trees and drop hard onto the water. Glen is the senior guide at King and Bartlett. His other job—his dead-of-winter work—is as a skidder driver, snaking sawlogs out through the frozen woods to be loaded onto trucks and taken to the mills. Physically, he's exactly what you'd imagine from either profession: six-foot-something and square-jawed, skin the color of toast, and shoulders and upper arms swelled from the year's labors. And whopping hands—log-wrestling, splitting-maul hands.

A large woman dressed in white from head to toe, Linda, hurries in from the kitchen, gliding like a butcher on roller skates, her arms cradling four huge plates covered with hot biscuits and eggs and bacon and perfectly browned potatoes. "It's thanks to my Aunt Ida," she yells from the kitchen when I ask her where she learned to cook like this. Aunt Ida, the housekeeper who lived with the family for seventy years, Ida the fairy godmother and keeper of the hearth, who could grow absolutely anything and cook absolutely everything.

"Did Roger have too much to drink last night or what?" Linda asks Glen, changing subjects as fast as she flips pancakes. Roger is a guest, the CEO of a large electronics firm in New York. "First two days," she says, filling me in as she eases down the last of the platters, "you couldn't calm the man down with a hammer to the head. He should be out here in the kitchen by now, driving me crazy."

"Keep your eye on Roger," Todd says. "He's a classic cliff dweller" (a more or less friendly guide term for people living in New York). "Tomorrow he'll stop talking so much. His shoulders will drop a little. By Tuesday he'll be so relaxed he'll practically be falling asleep in the boat." In the middle of this last remark Fred comes through the back door, sniffing the air as if to make sure the kitchen is running right, pulls up a chair next to mine.

"One thing you've gotta realize," he says, his small, deep-set eyes flaring above his copper-colored mustache, showing no sign whatsoever of last night's drinking. "The guys who visit here work damn hard nearly every week of the year. They come to get refueled. A little fishing. Maybe a drink or two and a little talk. When they leave, they're back on their feet again." An image flashes through my mind of these executives as boxers and Fred as their manager, rubbing their shoulders with the woods between rounds, feeding them a diet of clear nights and the cold smell of pine pouring through the cabin windows.

On my way out, I say hello to a large, pale man, walking briskly, hands in the pockets of a new pair of jeans, eyes straight ahead. It's Roger. He almost stops to chat, but in the end just slows a bit and talks over his shoulder, as if breakfast is an appointment and he's late. And being late isn't yet an okay thing.

Stuffed with breakfast and conversation, just like Joe

Knowles was by the grace of some other King and Bartlett cook more than eighty years ago, I grab my pack and set off through the woods. By reading Knowles's accounts, as well as by talking to a couple of old-timers who claim to be versed in his adventure, I've pierced together at least the first part of the wild man's route. My plan is to follow it out from the lodge, first heading northeast on an old tote road toward Beck Pond, then east across the shoulder of Bear Mountain toward Lost Pond, where Knowles hung out off and on for the first several weeks of his adventure.

For about the last twenty years I've had this fondness for going through wild areas, especially woods, off-trail, cross-country with map and compass. I started playing with it during college in southern Indiana, stumbling through the hardwoods of the Hoosier National Forest, got more serious out West, in the Sawtooth Mountains of Idaho. It's one of those things that's especially exciting right at the start, when you don't know what you're doing. The first few times you find the courage to take off through a mile or two of forest, you're as likely as not to find yourself locked in this overwhelming feeling that the compass broke, all the while this little voice saying you'd be a damn fool to depend on some flimsy needle surfing the earth's magnetic lines instead of trusting your own gut feeling that north is somewhere else altogether.

Years back, somebody with a lot of time on his hands actually had dozens of people walk through deep forest on a cloudy day to see if they could keep a straight line. Nobody could do it. Some went right and some went left, but they all ended up going more or less in circles. The experimenter said it was due to slight differences in the length of people's legs. I think maybe it's that our minds will do darn near anything to turn us off a path into the unknown.

Worse yet is that when you finally do break out into the open and it makes sense to pull out the map again, you start morphing those topographic lines into land features that have nothing to do with what they were intended to show and everything to do with the hill or cliff or stream drainage that happens to be right in front of you. And of course you only really need to do that once to be in a hell of a mess, and that's just what you keep reminding yourself out in the field.

Even today I wasn't trailing after Joe Knowles without recognizing the possibility of getting lost. What I didn't count on was being suffocated. When a moist northeastern woods is only thirty or forty years from the saw like this one, there's enough sunlight reaching the ground to grow vegetation thick as fur on a beaver's butt, and full of tangles. By the time I've gone a hundred yards, my visibility has dropped to a lousy fifteen feet. About every fourth or fifth step I trip over stumps or downed logs hidden by carpets of club moss and blueberry, several times actually falling, or else find myself mushing up to my ankles through sopping-wet cedar bottoms.

Skinny young balsam and maple are everywhere, their branches dripping and slapping, drenching me with dew. In other places the laurel is so thick that a greased Chihuahua couldn't make it through. Todd's story about Sir Edmund Hillary's recent visit to the King and Bartlett Camp is taking on new meaning. "Funny thing," he told me. "Hillary went out for a hike one afternoon. Came back saying this was the damnedest ground he'd ever tried to walk." It's the kind of abundance that can seem all-consuming—the Garden of Eden long after God left and fired the gardener.

I used to imagine all the forests of early America being like this—wild walls so thick and dark it was little wonder the Puritans saw the Devil hiding behind every tree. But it wasn't that way at all. In most of New England, old trees grew fat and well-spaced from a floor cleaned regularly by burns—some natural, some by native peoples managing the land for certain plants and wildlife. A Robin Hood forest, friendly to travelers on horseback, even those in wagons.

"Used to be we never cut a tree less than eight inches," a former lumberjack from Eustis told me, now in his seventies. "And we still had plenty of 'em big as sugar barrels. Open woods with big spruce and fir, maple, beech. Now the tree harvesters take everything in sight. That's why the water's goin' bad. Pools under the surface in these hard-clay-and-gravel bowls—sits there and gets sour, then the next storm flushes it into the creeks. Farther downstream you go, the more sour it gets." In addition to sweet water, there are a lot of other riches being lost in the rush to clear-cut the Maine woods. Native Americans are having a tough time even finding birch trees big enough to harvest bark for wigwams and canoes; black-ash trees used in basket-making are getting hard to come by as well, not just from clear-cutting, but from acid rain and other pollution.

Another hour and a half mile of lurching and stumbling, of swatting the growing mist of flies and mosquitoes, and I finally join the path up Bear Mountain. Just an old logging road, really, abandoned about ten years ago and already overgrown with a loose weave of shoulder-high maples. Much of the route is lined with middle-aged paper birch, each tree with wide ribbons of outer bark that have split and curled away from the trunk. As the sun rises in front of me the beams catch these strips of flagging full on, illuminating the russet-colored inner layer, making it glow, until the route up the mountain seems cradled by the light of a hundred red lanterns. Luminaria hung by the fairy folk to celebrate the cusp of summer.

Equally fine are the carpets of bunchberry, their whorled leaves scattered across the ground like a beach full of tiny green umbrellas, and the sweet spice of young balsam. Red-eyed vireos flit about looking for bugs, singing all the while, and white-throated sparrows are going on and on with that confounding lyric of theirs, something about "poor Sam Peabody, Peabody, Peabody." Far off in the trees I can hear the flutey music of a lone wood thrush—the song Thoreau said makes all men young again.

When I finally gain the shoulder of Bear Mountain I can see Spencer Lake in the distance, sprawling through a hundred wooded ravines. There was a time when sportsmen were willing to travel some twenty miles by motorboat, and another seven by rubber-tired buckboard, just to fish those waters. But today the place is largely ignored. On most mornings much of the surface remains unbroken by boats, a great sweep of calm shimmering in the summer heat. From here I opt for yet another slice of cross-country, this one through a much more mature growth of woods, manage to get lost, or at least confused for a time, and finally arrive at Lost Pond in the early afternoon on a shore thick with fir and striped maple, their feet wrapped in blankets of club moss, twinflower, and velvet-leaf blueberry. A loon sits rock-still in the center of the pond, glassy now, unruffled by even the slightest whisper of wind. Track lines from two different bears run along the shore, each weaving back and forth like the loose steps of children, pulled by curiosity from water's edge to flower patch to rotted log.

After supposedly having been lured to this pond by a game trail early in his adventure, Knowles claimed to have killed a black bear along the shore by hitting it over the head with a club and then skinning it, turning the hide into clothing; a picture of him in this skin—looking kind of like Tarzan in the throes of a midlife crisis—ran in newspapers across the country. Later on, when skeptics raised eyebrows about whether such a feat was possible, Knowles was incensed, offered to do it all over again, this time in front of witnesses. And so it was that some unfortunate, rather sleepy-looking black bear was brought in, which Knowles promptly conked over the head and then skinned, using nothing but a sharp piece of slate. The crowd was mighty impressed.

The problem was that after the show, as the spectators

were heading back out of the woods, someone spotted a crude cabin right here along the shore of Lost Pond. The structure appeared to be several months old, but Knowles said he'd never seen it before—a claim hard to swallow given that he supposedly camped here for several weeks. "I knew then he was lying," said Helon Taylor, seventeen, who later became superintendent of Maine's Baxter State Park. From there, rumors sprouted like saplings on a clear-cut: con-man Joe, not living the wild life at all, but cozied up in a crude cabin with reporter Michael McKeogh, who was busy concocting a book to make them rich, lighting fires with matches, drinking whiskey and eating cans of beans and stew. To be fair, none of the skeptics ever could explain why, after his adventure, when Knowles was examined by the physical director of Harvard, he showed a marked increase in fitness over when he went in. In fact, said an amazed Dr. Sargent, it was "a hundred and fifty points better than the hardest test taken by the football men."

I spend the afternoon shuffling around the fringe of the pond, eyes to the ground, looking for signs of old camps. There are cedar swamps and raspberries and laurel thickets to pick through, and pocket gardens of flag iris to relish, the latter dotting the damp ground with splashes of Prussian blue. Tiny springs walk out of the earth onto narrow paths of moss-covered stone. The woods here have the gentleness of age about them—loose huddles of red spruce and balsam and aspen, well lit, and the ghostly amber-and-ash-colored skin of yellow birch.

I've almost finished circling the pond when, at the southeast corner, fifty or sixty yards from the outlet, I find a number of cedar logs worked a long time ago with ax and saw. Getting down on my knees, I comb the clutter of fallen trees and layers of shrubs, and in time actually find remnants of an old trash pile: a coffee can, old bean cans with baling-wire handles, all but rusted through. Could this have been part of Knowles's trash pile? I take off my pack, slather on a fresh coat of bug repellent, settle down in the shade of the cedars among the rusted cans.

On my way west across Maine I took part of an afternoon to visit with eighty-year-old Deb Sylvester, whose family bought the King and Bartlett Camp some fourteen years after Knowles did his wild-man thing. Sitting here now I think of Deb, the way he used to run around these hills, this same pond, full of the woods and strong as an ox. During my visit we sat in his bachelor-pad house, scattered front to back with his woodcarvings, and in his bedroom, a workbench filled with an array of chisels and glue and sandpaper.

Deb was thirteen in 1927 when his dad and older brother decided to chuck the grocery business and buy the old King and Bartlett place, long after it had gone from a burgeoning timber camp owned by the Augusta Lumber Company to a hangout for well-to-do hunters and fishermen. "Mostly they was lawyers," Deb said of the guests. "A few bankers, but mostly lawyers. From New York and Boston and Pennsylvania." Deb still makes trips to King and Bartlett, and when I asked if those lawyers were much different from the guests he sees today, he nodded his head. "Back then they knew how to settle in and relax. Nearly all of them stayed at least three weeks, some for six. Today ya do something and forget it the next day, it happens that quick. We're greedy to do things. Wasn't that way then. Those guys took the time to enjoy."

After rummaging around in a bedroom closet for a few minutes, he came back with a box stuffed with old black-and-white photos. One was of a smiling, broad-shouldered, capable-looking woman, his mother, standing in front of the old camp post office. The woman who got up every morning at four o'clock to fire the woodstove and make pans of biscuits and hot bread to go with the pancakes and sausages and eggs for the guides and the help and the guests. Forty or more on any given summer day—so many that the guides had to take their meals in the woodshed. Then photos of

Deb at thirteen, grinning into a summer day with a string of fish in his hand—and another one, looking decidedly less enthused, standing beside the huge wooden drum of a spring-loaded mangle used to iron the bedsheets. "I hated that damn thing," is all he says, and by the way he sets the picture aside, I half wonder if he's planning to throw it into the trash the minute I leave.

During cold months young Sylvester kept three beaver trap lines going, each about fifteen miles long; every day he'd walk a different line, and by the end of winter he'd worn out another pair of snowshoes. One time, miles out at twenty below, he broke through beaver-worked ice on snowshoes, barely managed to crawl out and make it back home alive. "It was wild," Deb told me. "Wild just like I was." He said that in the summer he carried mail sixteen miles from Eustis into King and Bartlett, more often than not on foot since the only time the buckboards were running was when guests needed in or out. And even when they were running, a fella might just as well walk, given the boulder-strewn, bone-shaking road you had to endure. Truth is that Joe Knowles said the same thing, telling how the sixteen-mile-long ride over the King and Bartlett trail was worse than two months alone in the forest. At one point Deb handed me a picture of a buckboard running over enormous rocks, most of them sticking two or even three feet above the ground, the box tweaked and twisted at the most amazing angles. "I tell ya, you could hear that wagon comin' an hour before it got there."

Come the brutal cold of December the whole family went into camp to cut and haul the wood they'd need for the coming summer, then again in January to saw ice from the lake and put it up in sawdust—five hundred cakes, fifty tons. "A person who lives in nature like that takes the hard knocks. It don't give you no breaks. You learn to take care of yourself, and that makes you a better person. You learn to look ahead."

After a good hour of photos and even a little preachin' on the side, I decided to ask about Joe Knowles. Deb got up, shuffled over to a bureau in the bedroom and removed two old maps, came back and eased into his frumpy, cushioned chair.

"Well, there was these two guides," he said, unfolding the maps. "One was Douglas, from Eustis, and the other was Demmins, out of Flagstaff. They had a camp right near Spencer Lake, called 'Twin Camps'. What they told me was that they had extra clothes waiting there, so after Knowles stripped down and headed off on the trail he ran right over and got the spares. It was all planned ahead of time. There ain't no man in hell gonna go long without clothes with all those goddamned mosquitoes and black flies." Deb goes on to say that the guides also left groceries at Twin Camps, so at night Knowles could hike over and pick up his grub for the next couple of days—cans of stew and beans, even bottles of beer. "Two reporters for the *Boston Post* stayed there at King and Bartlett and wrote stories—stayed right there in a cabin named 'Granite State'."

I have to admit that all along I've been holding on to this secret wish that Joe Knowles really did what he claimed to have done . . . that even if the guy did get into it in the first place because of some beer-soaked bragging in a Boston bar, he still would have figured some way to pull it off. But right now, sitting at this pond thinking about Deb, whose entire life was a spirited dance with the wilds, somehow it matters less. More amazing than what Knowles did or didn't do was the amazing effect the mere thought of such an adventure had on millions of Americans—husbands and housewives in Scranton and Cleveland and Des Moines eagerly reading headlines about the wild man, sipping dreams of the woods with their morning coffee.

It was this woodland stage, as much as the man, that led university professors around the country to head to campus in the fall of 1913 with their minds clipped to Maine: Sociologists talked about founding nature colonies; biologists and philosophers spoke of hatching new departments—even entire colleges—devoted to teaching the lessons of the wilderness. Thanks to Knowles, even preachers were suddenly eager to whip heaven out of this outback, declaring that the real lessons of Christianity would be learned not through any man's sermons, but from outings in the woods. "Behold a sermon two months long for the people of the United States!" cried Herbert Johnson, celebrated pastor of Boston's Warren Avenue Church. Johnson said he wished those who worshiped gold could understand the underlying spirit of the wilderness. He spoke of how what Knowles did would make men and women across the country go into the woods (he couldn't have been more right about that), and in the woods they would stop and think. And the more they thought, the longer the flag would wave.

Some of the fever was a matter of timing. By 1913, the tang of cleverness sometimes associated with the Industrial Age had gone sour. Fully 20 percent of America's children, most of whom a generation earlier would have been farm kids, were wedged into commerce. As Joe sat on the shore of this pond scratching messages on sheets of birch bark, thousands of ten- and eleven-year-old girls were pulling sixty-two-hour workweeks in the textile mills—"scrawny examples of malnutrition," one writer called them—earning a miserable seventy-five cents a day. Every night in the hills of Pennsylvania twelve-year-old boys tramped home in the last light, scoured coal dust from their hands and faces from ten hours spent picking impurities out of crushed ore, coughed it up at the dinner table between bites of potatoes and greens. When Senator William Borah of Idaho introduced a bill to improve the lives of kids in the workplace, he asked the government to do for children what it had done some time ago for calves and pigs.

By the time Joe disappeared into these woods, real wages had actually dropped from what they were fifteen years earlier; for a lot of people holidays like Christmas and New Year's came wrapped in resentment, since they meant no work and no pay. Industries worked their people to a frenzy for nine months of the year, then shut down for the remaining months, leaving everyone unemployed. More than a third of all industrial workers suffered from tuberculosis, and much of that was blamed on poor living conditions. The most detailed study of the times said that over ten million Americans—nearly 15 percent of the population—were so poor they couldn't afford the food and clothing necessary to keep a body in sound condition.

Little wonder that stripping naked and heading off into the woods seemed like a good idea.

I'm back at the kitchen at a quarter to six. Linda is tossing seasonings across sheets of pork chops for tonight's dinner, while Lou Ann slides pans of bread in and out of the ovens. Before long smells like holidays are drifting through the screens, pulling both guides and guests through the side door to swoon and ask after dinner. To those they know and like the women feign a shortage of patience, fretting at them, treating them like little boys who need lids screwed on. "If you don't get out of my kitchen you can just go hungry," Linda tells Roger, the CEO from New York, who's standing in the corner with Glen, hands in pockets, grinning at the sudden attention. Glen hurries over for a cup of coffee and then he and Roger head to the back room, while Lou Ann pushes past me and out the door for a quick cigarette.

"Fred told me he'd give me a trip to Puerto Rico if I quit smoking," she tells me on her way out. "To hell with that. If I want to go to Puerto Rico, I'll just go." About then, Todd walks by, within easy earshot, an investment banker from Boston at his side; Lou Ann shrugs at the two of them, flashes a guilty smile. "Me and my mouth," she whispers, and then hurries off behind the lodge to light up.

"Okay. What did I do wrong?" Roger is saying to Glen as I make my way to the back room. He's referring to his having been skunked at fishing. From the tone of his voice, he's not upset, merely curious, as if he were choosing a conversation to go with his Scotch.

Glen thinks for a minute, considers the student. "Well, you know, being a big fish is kind of like being a kid in the projects. You survive by being cautious. Suspicious. Not trusting things you don't know. You find safe places, comfortable places, and that's where you spend your day. Fish don't come out for every stranger with candy in his pocket." This he follows up with a brief discussion of techniques, strategies they'll use tomorrow to increase the odds of coaxing out the big ones.

Roger just smiles. I get the feeling Glen is so important to Roger's experience that he'd probably follow him were Glen to go work at some other camp, the way the rest of us might follow a doctor to a different clinic in another town. It's not just that Glen's been out in the woods a lot; in Maine, such people are as common as river rocks. What's striking is how he's managed to hold on to whatever note of amazement nature slipped into his pocket when he was just a kid. Glen's clients find themselves enchanted because he's enchanted. On any given summer day you'd stand a decent chance of stumbling across Glen and some stockbroker on their knees in the pines, Glen pulling stories from a pile of bear shit steaming in the woods.

"Glen's like a curator in an art museum," Roger says. "He's not there to tell you to like or dislike the paintings. He just makes it easier for you to look."

Glen flashes a small grin, doesn't say anything. Maybe he's trying to imagine himself as curator of an art collection. In truth, the two men are like people from different countries, communicating with one another by drawing pictures on the backs of matchbooks. But they'll come back together in these same woods next year, and probably the year after that. And if not here, then somewhere else.

The morning begins with a leaky tire that can't be fixed. When the owner of the service station in Stratton finds he doesn't have the right size, he gives me his truck to go looking for one. Another shop down the highway doesn't have anything in my size either, though they do offer me some good advice about what the fish are biting on in Flagstaff Lake. Thirty minutes later I rumble back to the garage empty-handed, ask Jerry to put on the spare, head next door for a bite of breakfast.

The Stratton Diner on the morning of the fifth of July is like a slow day at the cemetery. The help looks so bedraggled and worn-down that out of sympathy I end up ordering things that don't take much work to prepare: a couple of fried eggs, cooked however, and a piece of ham. Phyllis serves up a mug of coffee so strong a little dog couldn't make a track in it, then sits back down with a friend in front of *The Price is Right*. The other waitress, Gena, slumps on a bar stool, elbows on a glass display case, a cigarette hanging from her fingers. She smokes it by pitching her whole body forward, taking a drag, and then rocking back again, like one of those plastic bobbing birds that tips its head in and out of a glass of water. Behind her is an old sign, yellowed and tattered at the edges: "This isn't Burger King. You'll do it my way."

Though this is the morning after the busiest weekend of the year, the gifts in the glass case don't seem to have been moving very well. The shelves are brimming over with potholders with the shape of Maine sewn into them, and tiny pillows, not six inches across, with embroiderings of moose. Someone has cut pictures of fish from outdoor magazines, shellacked them onto slabs of pine, and turned them into clocks. There are Maine mugs, pen sets, and birch-log candle holders. In the corner of the case is a big pile of just one book, self-published by a local author, titled *Meditations of a Christian Martial Artist*.

About the time my breakfast arrives, a round, balding guy in his late forties wearing a plaid shirt drops by for a cup of coffee. Phyllis and her friend manage a sluggish greeting, while on *The Price is Right*, Johnny Gilbert yells at someone to "Come on down!" The man tries to kid with them for a minute or two, gets nowhere, ends up sitting down at the table next to mine. We start talking, and I find out that he too has been both a logger and a guide, though now his business is repairing furnaces. "Can't circle a tree anymore without finding a guide," he says, clasping his cup with enormous hands, as if trying to warm up after that cold shoulder from the women at the counter. "It's a good way to keep from havin' to leave the woods." The more we talk, the more it seems clear that this guy, like all the others I've met, isn't just partial to any old patch of New England woods. It's the Maine woods that matter. The forest across the border in New Hampshire, no matter how much it may look the same, just isn't.

I finish my last bite of toast, agree to one last cup of coffee, then head outside to try a phone call to Garrett and Alexandra Conover. The Conovers own a guiding business two hours to the east, and their names have come up several times as people I should talk to if I'm serious about woods. Thankfully they're between trips, and we agree to meet at their home later this afternoon. When I get back to the table, my breakfast partner turns to me, a thoughtful look on his face.

"You know what you were sayin' before, how everyone you meet seems real loyal to Maine? Reminds me of a story. This fellow comes up from Massachusetts to marry a Maine gal. Kind of gets treated a bit different—folks are cautious about him. Things don't get much better for his kids; people don't consider 'em full-blood Maine either. Well, the day comes his granddaughter is born, so this fellow heads right down to the store, where all the boys are gathered 'round, and springs the news. 'At least my granddaughter will get treated like a native,' he says. This one ol' boy just shakes his head. 'Reckon just 'cause the cat has her kittens in the stove, don't make 'em biscuits'."

Chapter Three

Several miles east of Eustis the road brushes against a wild-looking mix of fir, birch, and maple. The woods are spreading, fattening, flowing down the face of every hill, overhanging ponds and streams, nuzzling the edges of farms and fields. In the ditches dozens of yellow tiger swallowtails rise and fall from the faces of flowers, unsure whether to eat or dance. Pure blue highway now, all twist and jitterbug. Flycatchers throw off loud, electric buzzes from the trees, as if the woods were shorting out under the weight of the July sun, and red-eyed vireos dash back and forth across the cracks in the road. Meadows are crowded with mats of bindweed and yarrow, and beyond them, along the edges of the woodlands, stream long, colorful runs of barberry, foamflower, and lily-of-the-valley.

Not just plants, in the scheme of things long past, but medicinals too. Crushed yarrow leaves to stem bleeding in the shops of the carpenters and blacksmiths and shipbuilders, lily-of-the-valley to strengthen the heart. Those in need of a laxative never had to look farther than a spoonful of dried bindweed root, and any Christian who'd been out carousing on Saturday night could rid himself of his bloodshot eyes in time for Sunday services with a quick wash of barberry water. (Berberine, the active ingredient in barberry, is still the main ingredient used to get the red out.)

I've been thinking a lot about where I should go, trying along quiet stretches of roadway to sort out exactly which woods to waltz with in the weeks to come. My first notion—and I swear there was a time I didn't think this way—was to weave the trip around the so-called last of the best places: the biggest sweeps of forest, the wildest, the oldest. Lousy idea. Not that there isn't a whack-on-the-side-of-the-head value to visiting the largest of what remains of our wildlands. But the celebrity status of such places can be a bit distracting, especially when all you really want is a certain old brand of quiet—smell the smells, visit with a few locals, head out for walks on land where it's easy to lose the path.

I decide that when I finish my visit with the Conovers the best thing might be simply to make for the south in a loose drift, then slowly wend north again, docking at that handful of places I remember from a long, long time ago, when I was just a kid: the hills of Appalachia. That patchwork of woods and thickets near my old hometown, in the corny flats of Indiana. Those dark, sweet runs of pine in the far north. The places that know me. The places I'm pretty sure will welcome me back.

Beyond the towns the houses wear a settled, comfortable look. Harsh winters have scoured coats of paint into pale versions of the originals—reds have gone to rose, navy to powder-blue. Most rest beside well-tended gardens, and owners with more than a pantryfull of produce offer it to passersby on tables made of planks and sawhorses. I lose count of the yards of peas and flowers, of strawberries, beans, and beet greens. Along with things edible there're tables of crafts—lots and lots of them. Some, including most everything having to do with fishing, are well down the road to tacky. But a surprising number are quite beautiful—quilts, bird carvings, pottery—giving another nod to the reputation Maine residents have long earned for creativity, for engineering a kind of backwoods Bohemia. It's obvious, said one historian, that in Maine there's an unmistakable impulse to create.

By the middle 1800s the state's remote forest towns were overflowing with art: paintings, songs and plays, poems and rhymes and verse. Even the itinerant preachers who rambled through Maine's backwoods seemed fond of serving up their sermons in rhyme. One clergyman rode into the town of Israel to announce the death of a prominent local woman, offering the news to the tune of "Yankee Doodle."

The Lord God he took his rod
–and shook it over Goshen;
And poor Miss Lowe was called to go,
–and death it was her po'tion.

Far from being offended, the congregation nearly erupted into a jig.

"Why, there's men in these woods that could write po'try as good as Longfellow and Emerson," said one old lumberman in 1927. "If only they was booked up enough." (It wasn't unusual for people who were booked up enough to dive headfirst into the outback of Maine, surface with a strain or two of clever verse, polish it up and serve it to the rest of the country. Carl Sandburg's acclaimed poem, "The Buffalo Skinners," for one, was an adaptation of an old song written and sung by Maine lumbermen.)

Verse was especially easy to come by around the logging camps. It was functional art at its best, as often as not used to describe the working conditions offered by a given timber company. All it took was a couple of backwoods bards passing around ditties about how crappy some camp boss treated his men—or even worse, how bad the food was—and the next season that company would find itself having a heck of a time finding good workers.

The sages of the late 1700s had predicted exactly such artistic flurries in the country as a whole, saying how Americans would rise to new heights of creativity simply by virtue of having rubbed elbows with the woods. Some historians say these predictions were nothing more than part of an inferiority complex—that we looked across the Atlantic at the accomplished cultures of Europe and Great Britain, felt desperate to find something of our own to be proud of, ended up settling for woods, mountains, and rivers because that was all we had. But that ignores the fact that pride in nature had been building for a hundred years. Americans were never so thickheaded not to realize that without their forests they never could have dreamed of becoming a country. From the earliest Colonial times our commerce rested almost entirely on wood: lumber for the sugar works of the West Indies, white-oak barrel staves to Madeira and the Canary Islands, pitch, tar, masts, shingles, and clapboard to England, and entire ships to Spain and Portugal. New Englanders used to recline around fireplaces so big it took an ox to drag in the logs (the average house burned twenty to sixty cords of wood a year), and still had plenty of clear, choice wood left over for fences and wagons, fish traps and mill wheels, tools, houses, churches, colleges.

It was the great sweeps of forest, cut and smoldered into charcoal, that gave us the ironworks needed to turn out cannon and rifles in the Revolutionary War. And speaking of the war, one of the first real skirmishes of the revolution took place off the coast of Maine, when the townspeople of Machias prevented a British ship from commandeering a shipment of pine wood; chased it down, captured it, decorated it with evergreens and renamed it *Liberty*. When the time came for a young America to think in terms of identity, of heritage, we almost always saw ourselves in terms of trees—plastering them across our state flags, stamping them into our coins, sewing them as panels on the quilts we pulled over us to keep warm at night. Trees as the raw music that would become myth, legend, religion.

At a little market near Guilford I stop to buy something for Garrett and Alexandra, end up with a bag stuffed full of fruit, as if their having spent the summer in canoes might have left them risking scurvy. Garrett's directions are the first I've received anywhere in Maine that actually work—no doubt a good sign for a guide. With thirty minutes to spare I park the van down the road from their house, near the dozing village of Willimantic, and wander down to the banks of Big Wilson Stream. It's a wonderful river, split here and there by alder-covered islands, stained to the color of tea by tannic acids, dropping toward Sebec Lake fast enough to allow a person to hum along with the rollers, slow enough for quiet pools to have formed behind every slab of granite. Hugging the rocks are plush cushions of jade-colored moss, and tucked among these, scaly tufts of liverwort—that mysterious plant that's not quite moss and not quite lichen, that in fact isn't tied to any known ancient plant group at all. When not laced with the scent of water, the air runs thick with balsam; I draw it in, recalling old tales of slipping balsam pillows under the heads of children to spare them bad dreams.

Despite having just come off a hectic trip, the Conovers look remarkably relaxed. It doesn't take ten minutes of talking to think of them as people of above-average balance, the kind who by either skill or environment manage to be composed in the midst of all sorts of craziness.

We meet at their combination office and workshop, a beautiful place finely crafted out of pine, tucked into the trees like it sneaked there in the middle of the night. Soon after I arrive, though, they lead me down several hundred yards of dirt path through the balsam and birch and hemlock, past clintonia and bracken and Indian cucumber, to their home, summer and winter—a twelve-by-twenty-four-foot wall tent on the bank of Big Wilson Stream. Against the far wall of the tent are curtained-shelves filled with rodent-proof containers of dry foodstuffs, a propane burner, and an icebox. Farther down is a woodstove, and beyond that, a bed draped with mosquito netting, shut off from the rest of the tent by a sheet of canvas. Oil lamps are strategically placed, and books abound—contemporary works of fiction, nature essays, and accounts of explorations—a few here beside us on the kitchen table, others piled on the counter and beside the bed. We eat a lunch of bread and fruit and cheese, drink filtered river water. The sun is falling full on the canvas, causing the entire inside of the tent to glow with the colors of a candle flame; between conversation we listen to the sound of the river, always that river, singing through the walls.

"We'd been going up there for years," Alexandra is saying, continuing a story she started earlier about a two-month snowshoe trip she and Garrett made over some three hundred and fifty miles of untracked tundra in northern Labrador, through the historic homelands of the Nascapi Indians, to Ungava Bay. "We'd been going up a month at a time, trying to learn everything we could from the native people. Of course at first they didn't trust us. But we were patient. We knew enough not to come right out and ask for teachers. To the Nascapi, that trip we did to Ungava Bay was as important as all the time we spent struggling with their language. They saw it as a willingness to learn the language of the earth, their homelands. When we got back, the people came up and felt our arms and ribs and laughed like hell because we were so skinny. But we were alive, and they'd been sure we were going to die."

When people first told me about Garrett and Alexandra, what intrigued me wasn't so much their love for the out-of-doors, but their passion for traditionalism. Besides having learned from the Nascapi of Labrador, for some twenty fourteen Garrett pushed hard for the Vermont Academy, for the sole reason that the campus had woods on three of its four sides.

It was Garrett's destiny to drive the counselor nuts. "I've narrowed down my choice of colleges to three," he announced one day during a senior meeting. "All in the northern Rockies. But the University of Montana—that's the one that really interests me." The counselor, who by now should have known better, asked why, so Garrett pulled out a Forest Service map and unfolded it across his desk. "Look, he said. "There are five wilderness areas close by!" When he admitted he hadn't given admission requirements or even course options much thought, the counselor put his head in his hands. "I thought he was going to cry," Garrett says, sounding a bit sorry even now. "Someone looking at my life might assume I always knew what I wanted. But there was no plan. What I had was a search image. All I knew was what was acceptable."

At one point the two of them depart to tend a phone call, leaving me sitting in the sun surrounded by the books and paintings, by the smell of balsam rolling through the open windows. I wonder how many guests fall in love with the symbols of these people's lives—the wall-tent home by the river, the crooked knives, the wood-and-canvas canoes. Especially if they're longing for place, if they're hungry for connection. It's easy to imagine being overcome by the kind of seductive thinking so often exploited by advertisers, the kind that promises new leases from the trappings of other lives. I can already see the television commercial or the magazine ad: Garrett and Alexandra out on a whitewater river deep in the boreal woods, paddles slick in the murky light. And a plug line: "Conover Canoes. When the river demands your very best." We think that maybe if we have a boat like that, we can know something of the qualities it takes to animate it. And so we go buy one for a small fortune, bring

years they've been devoted students of the last of the old-time Maine guides. What started as fascination has swelled into philosophy, a kind of creed that washes their days with a precious, enviable sense of place. Learned people, slipping gently toward middle-age in the shade of the Maine woods, tending their souls by flinging open windows into the past.

Both say that as teenagers, they were forever peeling back the layers of things—fields and woodlots and the backyards behind their homes in southern New England—trying to imagine what those places must have been like fifty or a hundred years earlier. Just the kind of soulful rummaging that in time would lead them to see the whole world as a work in progress. What most people think of as inanimate they see as having a life of its own. "Some people think we use wood-and-canvas canoes for environmental reasons," says Alexandra, "because we think that plastic is bad. It's not about that. We use them because they're like my grandfather's ax that's had three different heads and four different handles, yet it's still my grandfather's ax. These canoes, you can replace every piece, every inch of them. You can love them, have a relationship with them. They glow. They talk. And when you're done, you can pass them on to another generation.

"An old-timer comes up to me and says, 'Nice wooden paddle, but I'll show you one that will work a lot better, and I'll tell you why.' And what he's telling me is what Nick Ronco, a Penobscot Indian, told him, and what Nick Ronco was told by his parents. So what I'm getting is an age-old story about why this paddle works—not everywhere, but here in Maine, in this place, in these waters. There's a sense of humanity in that approach. It's positive. It's not against—it's for."

A pair of nuthatches flit past the door of the tent. A red squirrel pokes its head in, looks around, turns and leaves. We pour more hot water, sip another round of tea, listen to the chatter of Big Wilson Stream slapping against the rocks.

Alexandra is right, of course. What could be more suitable than a tool, designed and refined over thousands of years, meant solely for use in one region? There's so much common sense in it, and yet at the same time it goes so against our tendency, our obsession, to homogenize. I have to admit that such thoughts have seldom occurred to me, or for that matter, to most other people I've traveled with into the wilds.

"You can buy a bunch of high-tech stuff, wrap yourself in petrochemical clothing and go into the wilderness," Garrett points out. "But that just adds to the feeling that you're an estranged visitor. The source of your equipment is invisible—it has nothing to do with those mountains. You may or may not have a spiritual relationship with the landscape you go to, but I can guarantee that those things will slow down whatever emotional connection you have." He concedes that in certain places—above timberline, or in a heavily used preserve—a person uses things like backpacking stoves because they have to. But if he's traveling in Maine or the boreal forest, where it's appropriate to cut wood with an ax, that's what he'll do. "Those tools give me a whole skill tradition—a life I can build and grow with. If I can make a crooked knife which makes me an ax handle which makes me a canoe paddle, and I go to interior Quebec in a wooden canoe that I can fix, then I've got this enormous string, this web, that goes directly to the environment I'm in, that teaches me more and more whenever I use it. I can't imagine living without that kind of immersion."

We clear the table and walk the half-mile of trail back through the woods, rubbing elbows with the balsam and birch, finally arriving back at the main lodge. The inside of the building is trim, like the lines of a well-made canoe, warmed by the gloss of red pine floors and walls and ceilings of white pine. Great dollops of sun are falling through skylights in the cathedral ceiling. Watercolors of the north country hang from the walls, seeps of gray and blue, as well as Nascapi snowshoes, and a large, uncluttered map of Lab-

rador. At the rear of the main room there's an entire of books. Enticing, appetizing books, the kind that as a I spent long afternoons pulling from the dusty shelves of neighborhood library. Books like *School of the Woods, The North (Being the Account of a Woman's Journey Through Can to the Arctic), The River's End, Bob North by Canoe and Porta* and *Bob North with Dog Team and Indians.* On the very to shelf, out of reach, are twenty-eight musty green volumes of the "Annual Report of the Journal of Ethnology," 1881-1907.

Adjacent to the front room is a kitchen with stores of flour and dried fruit and vegetables, and a spacious, open workshop with stacks of canoes, and racks of ash and cherry stock that in Alexandra's skilled hands will this winter be turned to paddles. In the midst of all the provisions sits an old Wellsmore and Company piano, several flutes, a Supertone accordion. Garrett explains that every year several dozen neighbors gather here for a spring fling, with big pots of food and people playing music and dancing until dawn.

We settle down again in the front room, beside windows that open to the woods. The conversation turns to upcoming river trips: the Penobscot and the Chesuncook, and two hundred miles in central Labrador, through ice-water canyons, past herds of caribou, and wolves running in the black of the spruce forest. Alexandra's eyes are wide with the telling, as if a part of her has drifted away, is there already. It's a look I see often in children, rarely in adults. She looks much the same way a few minutes later when I start asking again about her childhood in eastern Massachusetts—about the forested nooks and crannies that by the time she was sixteen had become "the arm around my shoulder, the place where I went to feel whole."

"When we were young, we didn't have a clue as to why we went to the woods," says Garrett. "Young kids never do. But if you're real lucky, you learn to trust the hunger." With his parents' support to attend an alternative high school, at

it home and hang it in the garage, shuffle out to look at it when there's nothing on TV.

"I think it comes down to being in touch with yourself," Alexandra has said. "Being content with who you are. It so happens that we found that contentment in nature. But for someone else, it might come from art, from music or religion. The point of using a crooked knife—or of making a paddle or learning a difficult canoe stroke—is only this: that these things allow us to do something with care; they're merely the channels for our passion. Anything done with care leads back to the self. And it's from there that people tend to do things that matter most to others."

I tell them I'm curious about the men and women who come on their trips. What does a week on a river in the woods do for them? Is it really just a vacation, or something more like a rite of passage? Garrett says over the years he's noticed that people's sense of ease in the woods tends to be proportional to how they're feeling about themselves at the time. If someone comes on one of their trips short on self-esteem, he usually ends up spending the first couple of days worrying about how he'll be perceived by the group. Wild, unfamiliar landscapes make the problem worse because they generate uncertainty; and when you're already feeling shaky about yourself, giving up control to nature feels terrible. Any guide, he says, knows the symptoms: someone eating more or eating less, retreating to the tent as soon as camp is pitched.

I've talked to other outdoor leaders who like to apply what amounts to fireside therapy—group hugs, sharing circles, that sort of thing. Maybe it's the New England blood in them, but the Conovers never suggest that at all. They seem to think the best way to beat anxiety is to teach people how to be just a little more in control of their immediate environment. Learning to build a fire or to filter river water, they say, is a small dose of mastery. And with mastery comes a sense of contribution. And with contribution, people start weaving roots—first to the group, later to the surroundings. Out in the woods, being relevant means fetching water, finding kindling, pounding in a tent stake.

"After the trips," Garrett says, "I watch these former strangers exchanging addresses and phone numbers, and it occurs to me that for a lot of these people, there's no sense of community in their lives. Here, they've gotten a taste of it. They all put up a rain fly in the rain, and they all benefited from it. They talked at night around the fire about stuff, about life with a capital 'L.' There's this little tribal entity, born out of nothing more than five days together in the woods."

Sometimes people ask the Conovers whether they get bored running the same rivers year after year. "It's a sign of inexperience," Garrett says "—this notion that if you do something once, you know what that is. It's like a person. You don't get sick of them because you see them all the time. You love them more because they're always revealing more of themselves."

Part of Garrett's passion, I suspect, rests in the blissful knowledge that this particular home woods is in the toe of a boreal forest that stretches for hundreds of miles to the north and west. "One goal in all this learning," he confesses, "—first from the old Maine guides, now from the Nascapi—is that we're planning to take a multiyear trip, largely self-contained. I want to make our own moccasins when it turns from canoeing to snowshoeing. We want to be able to say, 'Well, here's where we're going to be until we have traveling ice.' And that place had damn well better be where the caribou are, because we're going to need a few of them. One day we'll walk out of the bush at Great Whale River, Quebec, four hundred miles west of where we started, and come face-to-face with the farthest-upriver native trappers. And we'll greet them in their own language. And right from the start, they'll know two things: One is that we're coming out of the bush with a body of skills that they remember if they're over forty; and two, that we've spent some time among their people, because we can speak their language. And that gives us light years more acceptance. Imagine if we stumbled into the village and said, 'Gee, where's your best snowshoe builder, because we want to learn to build snowshoes?' They'd say, 'C'mon, get out of here. We've already been bothered enough by you people.' And they have."

There seems to be one fairly obvious contradiction in the Conovers' lives. On the one hand, they live in a wall tent by the river, and on the other, they make a living taking city people into the woods—people who don't really have to be there—and charging them a fair amount of money for the privilege. They take from the culture's existing economic structure, while at the same time trying to live apart from it. I ask about this, and Garrett nods. "We've made choices. And those choices allow us to live outside those parts of the system that we find unacceptable. The truth is, that's a skill. You're supposed to do that; as Wendell Berry pointed out, you're obligated to do it. We're not hiding out. The books I write, the lectures I give, the town meetings I go to—the things our guests are able to take from a week with us—that's what I can do. And that's enough. Your highest calling is that thing which you're really good at. Don't exceed the bounds of your passion."

Building conversation with the Conovers is turning into another birch-bark wigwam; I hate to overstay my welcome, but on the other hand, it's awfully hard to leave. A hot, sticky afternoon begins to fade into a sultry evening. Standing on the front porch, I can smell every corner of the forest: the aspirin-like whiffs of birch bark, the dull lemon of leaves and grass, the scent of wet dirt, which is the olfactory equivalent of a motherly pat on the head.

On Alexandra's suggestion we head out for a bite to eat—down the road twenty miles, to Dotty's. When we arrive it looks like half the county is there, a wonderful collection of homegrown faces smiling over plates of steaks and hamburgers and fish, while fifteen or twenty of us stand in a line curling out into the mudroom, trying to jockey for a better view of a glass case spinning platters of cherry, chocolate mint, and banana cream pie. Perspiring waitresses squeeze in and out of the crowd like water balloons, seeking the easy paths through old men talking at tables on their way to the bathroom, out and around five-year-olds galloping up the narrow aisles.

It takes more than thirty minutes to get a table. With it comes a thin waitress in her early fifties named Jean, who in the midst of the craziness still finds time to make us laugh and call us "Honey." We turn in our orders, Jean takes back our menus and with a snap, tucks them under her arm, slips back through the crowd. Waiting for our salads, I ask Garrett and Alexandra about the clients who don't come, the ones who somehow hear about North Woods Ways and call up for more information, thinking its trips are something they're really not. Entertainment. Distraction. It's true that their brochures make it fairly obvious what to expect. Still, there must be some who don't get the message. Surprisingly, the question causes the first flash of distress I've seen in Alexandra all afternoon.

"Oh, we get those all right," she finally says. " 'I want to see at least six or seven moose,' they'll say. Or, 'I know there are bugs up there. Will any of them bite me?' Or, 'How many days of rain will there be next September?' It's terrible," she says, crunching a piece of ice, her voice a strange mix of aggravation and worry. "I know that in this country this is heresy, but Disney's version of nature scares me. Scares me like a Southern Baptist opening the front door and finding the porch filled with devil-worshipers. When that's your only experience, you tend to see nature as something quantifiable, prepackaged. And pretty soon your most pressing concern is trying to get your expectations met."

She says I'd be surprised at the degree to which even people who do come on their trips are tied to the need for predictable experience. "If we're on a trip and we say we don't know where we're having lunch—which is almost always the case—some of them will get frantic. It has nothing to do with appetite, because when we ask if they're hungry, they say no. They're just obsessed with having this target, this concrete expectation. Sooner or later one of us will have to say, 'Oh, it's just two and a half miles now, this perfect place on a bend in the river. We'll be there in just over an hour.' And then everything's fine again."

In truth, Garrett and Alexandra aren't the only ones in these woods worried about this growing sense of impatience, of unease, in their clients. Another couple living just up the road, who own one of the oldest tourist camps in the state of Maine, say much the same thing. Only, they blame a lot of it on the fact that people have been deluded by television to expect that nature will provide them with one big parade of miraculous events. When it isn't like that, they leave their little cabin on the lake and scour the countryside in search of outlet malls.

"If I can just get them to pull the rocker up to the edge of the porch and stare at that lake for one hour," the woman says, "then they're okay. They feel wonderful. But believe me, that gets harder every year."

Chapter Four

The next morning I snap a couple of photos of Garrett and Alexandra for the fridge at home, and then I'm off, rolling south on a web of sloop-shouldered roads, past ditches lined with bindweed, down valleys filled with pulp, the smell of it turning, moiling, like a crock of sourdough batter left out in the heat. In places, the woods draw back, yielding the ground to long runs of potatoes; across the fields are old homesteads, easy to recognize by the pairs of maples or oaks growing outside the front doors of the main houses. "Husband-and-wife trees," they used to be called, and the ritual of planting them was a celebration of intent, a pledge to place. Soul trees presiding over lives wedded to the woods: over fathers and brothers splitting fence rails with hickory mauls; and in spring, over women who sat patiently folding strips of basswood into berry boxes. Shade for daughters straining at oak churns to make their first batch of butter; for young boys sitting with knife in hand and tongues wagging, carving out apple-butter paddles for their mothers' birthdays.

My plan is to sooner or later end up over a thousand miles to the south, in the big woods of the southern Appalachians. But for now, for at least the next several days, it seems best to travel much as Garrett Conover described his life moving—armed not so much with a plan, as with just a search image. Of course one of the great things in waltzing the woods is that you can stand at twenty paces and toss a dart at a map of the eastern United States and more than likely, you'd hit some grand tale of history or prehistory born of trees; nearly every back road, every woodlot, every small town still carry the echoes of that past.

Except for a curious abundance of Italian sandwiches, the road food is about what you'd expect in a land of woodlots and spuds. Tucked between the big, double-decker houses that front Main Street in the village of Mexico are broilers and mashed potatoes at the Chicken Coop Class A Family Restaurant ("No Brag, Just Fact"), hot coffee and warm apple pie at the Going Home Cafe. If you choose to eat on the road, as I do today, for company you can count on Preacher Paul, the FM apostle from WWOR-FM, who begins his afternoon talk with pleasant, blue-sky thoughts of the hereafter—easy to digest with my pint of potato salad. Later on he starts wandering into the land of the strange—notions to pick the chicken out of my teeth by—cryptic, confusing ideas, like the need for preachers of the world to find the Alpha and Omega of grace.

Following Preacher Paul, and just in time for dessert, is a health show that starts off with Bob calling from New Jersey to tell us listeners he's cured all that ails him—and I'm telling you, Bob was one sick man—through the miracle of Bogdana Power Creme for the feet. I glance at the pharmaceuticals rolling by the window—sweet clover for flatulence, mullein for asthma, dandelions for regularity—and have to admit that all of them put together couldn't begin to do that.

The landscape of southwest Maine and northeast New Hampshire is choppy—dimples and roller-coaster runs of corduroy covered in mixed woods. This is prime moose country, a fact the state of New Hampshire doesn't want you to forget. "Brake for Moose," says a sign at the border. "It Could Save Your Life. 211 Collisions." Moose are among my very favorite animals—so much so I sometimes have this weird notion of being protected against ever hitting one. Still, I have to admit that plowing into one with a Chevy van would be a horrible thing, a frightful omen foretelling the sourest of summers. To be safe I slow way down, switch off babbling Bob from New Jersey and focus all my attention beside the road—on these sweet, dark runs of maple and spruce, on wetlands near campgrounds wearing names like "Timberland" and "Pine Knot" and "White Birches." Sure enough, in a few miles I spot a young male moose standing up to his kneecaps in copper-colored water, scooping up water lilies. A red caprice is parked beside the road, and a large, fair-skinned woman is leaning out the window nearly to her waist with a disposable camera, snapping one picture after another.

South of Highway 2 begin the granite swells of the White Mountains—clearly, of all the high country in New England, the most dazzling route to the sky. No forest in America has been host to more of both the yearning and the careless abuse that describe our relationship with wild places than this one. From a pioneer point of view it started in the late 1700s with a cast of gnarly, unflinching settlers hacking clearings out of the woods to graze a few milk cows, to grow the grains and summer squash that would steam on maplewood plates next to servings of moose and passenger pigeon. With no sawmills nearby, building materials had to be fashioned with an adz and a broad ax; likewise, since there were no grain mills, Indian corn, wheat, rye, and barley were turned to grist by hand, as often as not pulverized in wooden mortars.

The basics were incredibly hard to come by; tough old Eleazar Rosebrooks, for one, thought nothing of hauling a bushel of salt eighty miles to his home near present-day Colebrook. Even if you did manage to actually carve out a productive farm here, there was the devil to pay when it came to rounding up enough seasonal help to work it. The best solution was to build a cider mill out in the barn. That way you could bribe your workers with rations of applejack.

But of course this was the frontier, after all, and on all frontiers, mulish perseverance was as common as chickweed in a ditch row. What made the White Mountains unique was the way they breathed inspiration into another, completely different aspect of the national personality: an amazing sixty-year obsession with putting God back into nature, and nature into God.

Fundamentalists today like to banter about how Christianity had such a firm hold on young America. But what they don't say is that the Holy Book of the times was the woods and the mountains—more useful, thought most people, and every bit as unfailing as the Bible. By the early 1800s you would've been hard-pressed to find any brand of religion, thoroughly reformed or steadfastly orthodox, that wasn't smitten with the notion that nature was irrefutable proof of the Divine; even for the most literate, scholarly theologians, the boundaries between the notion of God having created nature and God *being* nature had all but dissolved.

From 1790 to 1820, long before the nature-loving Ralph Waldo Emerson's philosophies began rooting in the psyches of New Englanders, you could warm a pew in almost any church from Long Island Sound to Boston to northern New Hampshire and as likely as not, you'd hear the preacher talking about "sermons in the stones," about the genius of forest and tides and stars, of the need and wisdom of seeking God in the songs of woodland birds. It wasn't sportsmen, but clergymen from Boston and New York who made up the lion's share of early travelers in the deep woods of New Hampshire and Maine, some of them returning time and again, ever on the lookout for ways to build better links between nature and the soul.

Given all that it's not surprising that Americans would serve themselves extra does of the Divine not like Europeans did, through the breathy paintings of a Grünewald or a Botticelli, or the sculptures of Ghiberti, but in the works of landscape painters. For years there was the most pious gaggle of landscape artists imaginable tramping the New England countryside, especially the White Mountains, talking in hushed tones about what they called the "Scripture of Art," offering their fledgling students lessons that were every bit as anchored in catechism as in technique.

Men like Thomas Cole, who routinely wandered the rocky ravines of these mountains looking for the perfect scene; on finding it he'd take out his flute and play soft rifts of music—his way of speaking to the landscape, he explained—and only then would he settle in to sketch. Which is how he created pieces like the magnificent *View of the White Mountains*. Out of a ragged, tattered stump rises a young elm firmly binding heaven to this sprawling run of comely highlands. (In Christianity, stumps were a symbol for mortality, but in later America they were used to represent the destructive forces of civilization.) It was just one of hundreds of painterly appearances for the elm, which was fast on its way to becoming the tree of choice for denoting the promise of freedom in the New World. In the middle distance of Cole's painting are two small figures walking a broad path into the shadows, ultimately bound for a brilliantly lit slice of wild valley. The valley, then, cradles the feet of Mount Washington, topped by a soft halo of clouds. We are still in Eden, Cole said. "And the wilderness is yet a fitting place to speak of God." Other great artists—Bierstadt, Church, Durand, Frankenstein, Oakes—would also come to this place. And that most famous of all American art movements, the Hudson River School, would be known first as the "School of the White Mountains."

Evening is well along when I finally park the van off a weed-choked two-track road south of U.S. 2 and rid myself of the last of the coffee from the Going Home Cafe. The air is thick with the smell of pine; nearby, two long-eared owls hoot at one another from out of the blackness. It's a clear night, and high above me is the figure of Hercules, spinning in a dozen points of white starlight, his bow ever poised to fire on the neck of Draco the Dragon. Farther south the archer is similarly engaged in an attack on Scorpius, and near him, the good doctor Ophiuchus continues his wrestling match with the serpent. When one embraces Greek mythology the entire summer sky becomes a cosmic battlefield. And yet there are other tales that lend a welcome benevolence to the stars, that in fact tie them to the earth in such a way that the cosmos seems less a collection of parts or personalities than a single whole. The Egyptians said the goddess Nut blessed the earth each night by releasing celestial milk for the nourishment of trees and plants—hence the name "Milky Way." Algonquian myth speaks of colossal New England pines serving as ladders into the heavens, where heroes could pull themselves into the loveliest, most peaceful of all the worlds.

My last recollections of the evening are the sounds of the long-eared owls still gossiping with one another in the woods and the occasional snap of a twig beneath the foot of a whitetail deer. I drift off to sleep half hoping for visits by some of the ghosts of these White Mountains—maybe Thomas Cole, or the nature-loving Reverend Thomas Starr King—half hoping they'll invite me up to spend the night in the howling winds on Mount Chocorua, or farther west, listening, as they often did, to the sound of God rumbling in the belly of Tuckerman's Ravine.

After fifteen years and some three hundred thousand miles traveling in this van, the routine is clear, unambiguous. Fire up the Coleman stove to heat water for coffee and oatmeal (or plug the coffeepot into the cigarette lighter if I'm in a hurry), grab a lawn chair and set it up in some strategic place to catch the first rays of the morning sun. If Abby the traveling cat is along, which she often is, before I even get free of the sheets my glasses are on and I'm scanning the floor for half-eaten mice lying next to the bed, because in truth there's no nastier way to start the morning than by stepping on a half-eaten mouse in your bare feet. (Heaven forbid if I wake up and realize I've forgotten to stuff towels in all the mouse escape routes before going to bed—the gap under the refrigerator, the crack at the edge of the storage door beneath the bed. Because that means I probably have a live mouse holed up somewhere, and that part of the morning will be spent trying to find it and shoo it out when Abby isn't looking.)

The breakfast dishes, which on most mornings are all of a Sierra cup and a spoon, are washed and rinsed with the remaining hot water, then dried and packed in their appointed nooks in the cabinet above the refrigerator. The bed gets made, the fridge turned on, and the passenger seat—which also serves as the nighttime reading seat—is swiveled and locked back in its normal position, facing forward. Cooler and lawn chairs are loaded, the stove slid into the center cabinet, the remaining coffee placed in the cup holder on the driver's door. I can do it in my sleep.

Living out of this van is one of those things in life where the doing is every bit as good as the fantasizing about it. I never outgrew it. Camping out in woods, cruising through little towns in a vehicle small enough to parallel park, is the blue-collar American version of the European Grand Tour. The only thing that's really changed over seventeen years is the number of miles I'm willing to go on any given day. I used to get a strange kind of satisfaction in just driving—seven hundred, eight hundred miles a day if I had to get somewhere, the last two hundred with the radio spilling out a bizarre assortment of talk shows, working through cups of burned coffee from a parade of bleary-eyed clerks at the all-night gas stations. But these days there are times when even a hundred miles are too much. Middle-age has brought with it a longing for more conversation with strangers, more back-road slices of pie, more calling it quits early to sit in the sun with a book and a bottle of wine.

But there's something else, too. Converting this vehicle from a panel truck into a rolling house and office was the last real project I did with my father. We froze our butts off at it, January in Indiana, working a couple of hours and then running into the house to thaw out our fingers. Up until that point I'd been neck-deep in one harebrained adventure scheme or another—sailing for the Bahamas in a rickety boat, hopping freight trains—never paying all that much attention to my father's world, much of which turned on the amazing ability he had to make things with his hands. While working on the van, I discovered that somewhere along the way—probably when I was a kid standing next to him in the basement, building a hair hydrometer or a model furnace or some other hoo-haw for the science fair—I must have soaked up something after all. It was good to uncover it with him right there, standing at my side.

Eighteen months after we drove the last screw into these cabinets on a cold October morning at a job site in Plymouth, Indiana, he volunteered to walk out on a high metal roof to see if it was free of frost, safe to work on, slipped and fell sixty feet. We buried him at the edge of the cemetery near a grove of oak trees; Indian summer ended early that year, and I remember the ground was already strewn with thousands of leaves, rattling in the cool breeze, trapped in the tall blades of grass and wanting to fly.

I've decided to pass on a trip down State Highway 16 through the heart of the White Mountains and go east instead, to Franconia, to the old farmstead of Robert Frost. Just fifty acres of pasture and trees, but arguably the most meaningful place Frost ever lived. It was the farm with the dazzling view from the front porch of the Franconia Mountains—the farm he decided he just had to have, and so one spring day he went up to the owner, who was out raking his yard, and suggested to Herbert Willis that he move next door instead. And so Willis did.

I like Robert Frost for lots of reasons besides his poems, not the least of which was the way he looked as an old man: face chiseled like White Mountain granite, frocks of white hair forever stuck in the spin cycle. I like the fact that while he received some forty honorary degrees, he never got a diploma. He joked about that a lot, claiming he was a man educated by degrees. I like that Frost was on some days lazy and on others industrious, sometimes jaundiced, cynical, and at other times front man for Pollyanna. An old friend of the poet described him as being hesitant to do things just because they were supposed to be done. He wasn't willing, said the friend, to become a decent board instead of remaining a growing tree. But maybe what I like most about Robert Frost is that he knew enough to come to a certain patch of New Hampshire farm and woodlot to save himself—to "fix" himself, as he put it. And what could be more wise, either in his time or ours, than knowing where to go to get fixed?

Along the way I pass the Appalachian Trailhead parking lot, which looks like the side yard at the Baptist Church on revival Sunday, though the jumble is far less Buick and LaBaron than Subaru and Cherokee. From this spot on the Moose River there's an almost endless tangle of trails taking off through the birch and ash and spruce and maple, climbing south, toward the heart of the high country. Randolph Path and Sylvan Way, Short Line, Air Line, and Valley Way. Howker Ridge and Watson Path, Amphibrach and Cliffway—gateways to a world of gentle forest glens and boxcar-sized boulders, waterfalls and ravines, and of course to that world-famous toss of alpine summits, each one shorn and shredded by some of the stiffest winds in America.

The sun is well up by the time I cross the Israel River, named for Israel Glines, a traveler who happened to camp here sometime in the mid-1700s. Nothing against Israel. And nothing against his brother John either, who stumbled across a watercourse ten miles to the west at about the same time, Johns River. But I've always appreciated landscape names that give some hint about the look of the place, maybe about what goes on there. Androscoggin River, from the Abenaki—"fish-curing site." Or the Mahoosuc mountain range, thought to have been derived from another Abenaki word, meaning "dwelling-place of the hungry animals." Before Israel Glines came along the native people knew this stream as Siwoog-i-nock—"a place we return to in springtime." Even the name "White Mountains" alludes to the snow that lies on the summits for much of the year.

When I finally reach the Frost place it seems overcome with summer. Out front poppy blooms crowd the slanted mailbox post, swaying back and forth on their long stems, dizzy-looking, as if they're about to collapse in the heat. Before I even set foot on the place I decide the front porch is perfect, the kind of porch where you could go out to the glider with a glass of lemonade at two in the afternoon and not wake up again until dinnertime. Neighbors told of spotting Frost out here on warm afternoons, his bare feet sticking through the loose tangle of morning-glory vines that ran from the rail to the roof. Either there, or out walking in the woods—"farming," he called it. "Dumped down in paradise we are, and happy." At the small barn behind the main house a young man in shorts is sitting in the shade reading a novel, taking money now and then from the trickle of visitors, getting up every twenty minutes to restart a video about the life of Robert Frost.

For the most part, the house is just what you'd expect for a rural New Englander. Yankee-spare, uncluttered, functional. But past the living room and up a narrow rise of oak stair treads, each one ground to cups by an endless parade of visitors, there's a collection of nooks that seem steeped more in pleasure than in practicality. To the east of the stairway landing is a simple dormered room wrapped in paisley-patterned wallpaper, washed in light from a casement window overlooking the poet's three favorite White Mountain peaks: Lafayette, Lincoln, and Liberty. Frost's writing desk sits in the spillway, just as it did some eighty years ago, the surface faded and slightly warped, traces of his fondness for keeping the window open even in the face of blowing summer rains.

On the other side of the narrow, honey-colored landing are more windows, these facing west, offering views into a cluster of trees crowded against the far side of a tiny yard. They include a massive white pine and a yellow birch, standing like old guards at the gate of what was for Frost a cherished run of mixed hardwoods—a place of fringed orchids and rose pogonias and ovenbirds, and old beech trunks with initials carved in them to mark the corners of the property lines—so called "witness trees"—all of it to be savored and turned to verse.

Suddenly I'm itching for a closer look. I head back down the stairs, past the closed room where the current poet-in-residence is hiding out, readying himself to do a reading for visitors out in the barn later in the day. In the living room is a couple in their sixties, the woman reading interpretive brochures to her husband, who scans the room through the bottom of his bifocals, not saying anything at all. The woman seems concerned when I leave, staring after me as I walk off the front porch and around the house, worried maybe that I might be heading off to some event she hasn't heard about; later, entering the woods on the Poetry Trail, I happen to glance back and notice they're following, confused looks on their faces.

It doesn't take ten steps for the harsh August heat to yield to the forest, for the world to move from a parched lawn into a sweet tangle of foamflowers and cowslips, violets and interrupted ferns. The humidity is incredibly high today, and the air hangs on my skin like wet wool. It was of this and other nearby woods that Robert Frost often told of hearing the call of a dark, wild voice—a voice he was forever tempted to answer but never did, passing it up time and again for various deadlines and commitments. For the same miles that most of us think we have to go before we sleep.

Yet, in the 1940s, Frost put on his rambling shoes and headed off up a small forest stream on a poetic journey into the unknown, gathering images for a piece called simply, "Directive." It's in that poem he seems most willing to step outside the polar views Americans had long held about their wildwoods, either insisting they be flooded with hope, as Emerson did, or seeing them as some kind of savage foe. In "Directive," Frost took on an older, probably wiser view of the forest, not unlike those spun out by ancient fairy tales, wherein the woods were uncertain places with thorns as well as flowers, places where people routinely ended up getting terribly lost and then finding themselves again. Frost seemed to be saying that while there was deliverance to be gained from the woods, getting it meant we first had to accept that nature would spin life in ways and for reasons completely beyond our understanding. If we chose to keep using the forest as canvas for rendering the human condition, then at some point we needed to muster the courage to paint the shadows, to say "Yes" to things like age and sickness and death. The poem ends without fanfare at the head of the stream, the narrator taking a cold drink of water from a broken cup. No rosy moral. No tidy endings to warm the storyteller on the long walk home.

I'm several hundred yards into the woods, reading a copy of a Frost poem posted along the side of the trail, when I hear heavy breathing. It's the couple from the house. The woman is flushed, and her husband is having a miserable time with his glasses, which keep sliding down the sweat on his nose. It turns out they're from Ithaca, taking the long way home after visiting a spanking-new grandson in Connecticut.

"Our daughter told us about this place," the woman says, sweeping her eyes upward to take in more of the woods. "She teaches poetry, and oh, she loves Robert Frost."

"What do you think of it?" I ask her.

"Oh, it's beautiful . . . it's just . . . well, I had this notion of Frost being a happy-go-lucky sort, not a care. But I was reading some of his poems out loud in the car on the way here—see, Jack likes me to read while he drives—and I don't know, it seems he was kind of troubled." And then she looks up at the trees again, like she expects to find the answers up there in the arms of the maples.

I wonder about the trees.
Why do we wish to bear
Forever the noise of these
More than another noise
So close to our dwelling place?
We suffer them by the day
Till we lose all measure of pace,
And fixity in our joys,
And acquire a listening air.
They are that that talks of going
But never gets away;
And that talks no less for knowing,
As it grows wiser and older,
That now it means to stay.

My feet tug at the floor
And my head sways to my shoulder
Sometimes when I watch trees sway,
From the window or the door.
I shall set forth for somewhere,
I shall make the reckless choice
Some day when they are in voice
And tossing so as to scare
The white clouds over them on.
I shall have less to say,
But I shall be gone.

I realize there are a lot fewer trees in northern Vermont than the beauty strips along the highways would suggest. Even so, it's still a state where it's easy to stick your head out the window at sixty and hear long runs of birch and spruce and maple singing the old songs of the hills. It's the trees that swell the uplands of Vermont far beyond their actual size, a sleight of hand where green light and shadow wax the summits and saddles until the whole world seems to be taking cues from the roll and rhythm of the heights.

I don't quite understand how, after the ravages of heavy timbering through the early 1900s, Vermonters managed to broker what looks to me like an above-average truce with the land—to see their woods as heritage, the way New Englanders used to talk about them. The few people I know here seem nearly unable to rake the yard, feed the cat, buy the groceries, without an occasional look over their shoulder up to these sweeps of nature, quietly acknowledging that at least a little of what keeps their lives in bloom rises in these woods, these cedar bogs and fence rows and sugarloaf hills.

I push on farther than I should, all the way to northern Massachusetts, finally pulling in late in the afternoon to a campground at Clarksburg State Park. Alyssa is the ranger here, and though she's barely twenty-one she looks plumb worn out. Tufts of black hair have strayed from under her hat and lie tousled against the frames of her glasses; there are beads of sweat glistening on her forehead and above her lip. She tells me she's just finished refereeing a bunch of grade-schoolers who were cussing up a blue streak near Site 59, freaking out a lone woman camper in her sixties. "Sometimes it's just baby-sitting," she says of her job. Especially on the weekends. "People tend to think of this as a pretty safe place. Let the kids roam. No need to get up from the fire except to grab another beer." It's a blue, blue-collar campground, she explains, most times filled with people who can't afford to travel far from home. Alyssa loves seeing the place full. "It's good they want to come. You won't believe this, but I went out on a date with this guy a couple of weeks ago; he'd never even been to the woods. Next week I'm taking him out for his first picnic! Now that's sad."

Alyssa informs me that at the end of a narrow, half-mile-long path through the hardwoods, is a large pond, and a beach. On hearing that I pay my camping fee, wish her luck, jump into the van to wiggle into my swimsuit and sandals. Coming from Montana, I'm used to entering swimming holes with breath held and every muscle above the thighs held tight, as if preparing to be hit with a two-by-four. But here the water is tepid, and I can swim out far from the shore and float and dive and generally lolligag around until my skin puckers. Which is just what I do.

It's near dark when I head back across the beach toward the woods. Along the way, a man leans patiently over two boys, maybe eight and ten, the younger one upset at having discovered a leech clinging to his leg. "Just pick it off, Matt," he tells the boy. "But Dad, don't they suck your blood?" Matt's brother wants to know, his eyes wide with alarm. "Well, after a while," the man admits. "But I'll tell you, you'll look high and low before you find a better fish bait than that." Amazingly, that pleases Matt to no end, and after watching for a few more seconds, he calmly peels the leech off and tosses it into the woods. I hurry my step, duck behind the first good-sized white pine I come to, pull down my trunks for a full-blown inspection.

Chapter Five

To leave New England without taking in the white pines would be like going to France and eating out of vending machines. White pines were everything. Straight, clear wood, and tall enough to grant the favorite wish of every shipbuilder in the world: to make masts again from single trees. The pines called to English explorers like sirens to sailors, like the smell of baking bread pulls at the hungry. England had become a woodless nightmare. People scavenged the commons of branches and kindling like hungry mice vacuuming crumbs from the bottom of a bread tin. In some parts of the country firewood prices were doubling every nine or ten months; the poor were left to beg for bread and cheese, to warm themselves by burning dried grass and cow dung, weeds and tattered mats of straw. When there was nothing left to eat and nothing to offer the flames, many died of pneumonia, or if they were especially lucky, in their sleep, from exposure. Women struggled to cook on fires made of twigs no bigger than pencils, and at night, families huddled together in bed like cats in a cold barn. Most of what trees were growing at the time were securely locked up in the royal forests, and whoever pilfered them did so at risk of being severely beaten.

It's easy to see how the woods could have vanished. All those timbers needed to shore up coal mines and make sluices and waterwheels for the mills that ground the grain and stamped the tin, that made the paper and pushed the bellows on the blast furnaces. Trees for barrels to ship flour and sugar and salt pork, bark for tanning leather on saddles and harnesses, potash for making everything from glass to gunpowder to soap. Saplings as hoops for the hop growers, and the woods themselves as the garden that grew the physician's herbs. Two thousand oak trees, big ones, to make a single warship. Sixteen cords of wood for a ton of iron, or about twenty-two thousand cords a year for a single average-sized factory. Fifty cubic feet of trees to fire a couple thousand bricks, forty times that for one ton of salt.

And always this or that royal family, either jealously guarding the woodlands (Richard II made it illegal for those in the lower classes to even own snares or hounds, as hunting was a "sport for the gentle"), or squandering its coffers, selling off the woods at a pittance for quick cash. If there really was a Robin Hood bedeviling the government, stealing from the rich and giving to the poor, he'd have had to be awfully good at hiding out, since by his time, Sherwood Forest was barely five miles by five miles. (Not to say he couldn't have done worse. In a lot of formerly wild places in England the "merry men" would've been reduced to cowering in hedgerows.)

Given all this, it comes as no surprise that explorers and settlers alike would walk through these forests drunk on the mere sight of them. "Here is a good living for those that love good fires!" one exclaimed. "A poor servant may afford to give more wood for timber and fire than many noblemen can afford to do." From Maine south to Florida and west to the Mississippi Valley—in all, more than a million square miles of forest.

It isn't that America didn't head off in much the same direction. But almost from the beginning, there were balancing factors that kept the desire for preservation galloping close behind the willingness to plunder. Some of it simply grew out of the deep horrors of the wood shortages in England. Many of the colonies, especially those south of the Merrimac River, reserved large tracts of forest as commons and forged strict laws against overcutting. Plymouth Colony had a timber-conservation law on the books by 1626, and less than thirty years later so did several small towns in the northern woods of what would become the state of Maine. William Penn suggested that one acre of trees be preserved for every five acres cleared.

Another, equally powerful balancing factor had to do with America having been planted at a time when nature was seen as a Divine gift—a sure nod from God about the spiritual and physical greatness waiting for us all. Long before we were ever a country, it was a common opinion that squandering woods was displeasing to the Creator, "Who abhorreth all willful waste and spoils of His good creatures." Still more of the urge to preserve came from that fanciful stew pot of dreams and visions spawned by nothing more than living day-to-day with the woods. And that was the most enticing of all.

Christians had stormed across Great Britain hundreds of years earlier armed with heavy metal—axes to chop down the sacred groves of the pagans, swords to skewer those reluctant to convert. Yet after centuries of such abuse the church had relatively little conversion to show for it. So in the year 601, Pope Gregory raised a white flag. In a letter to the Abbot Mellitus he told his charges that instead of trying to abolish the old pagan nature sites, the faithful should instead work to consecrate them. And that was what finally allowed Christianity to root. Statues of saints and the

Virgin sprouted under the branches of the remaining old spirit oaks, beside the sacred rivers and lakes. Enchanted wells came into favor again, their water blessed and used in baptisms—a practice that so closely mirrored the Celtic ritual of sprinkling newborns with well water that nobody even blinked.

In America, on the other hand, Christianity arrived thoroughly entrenched, and ended up itself being converted—not by other faiths, but by the impact of living with our backs to the wilderness. It isn't as crazy as it might sound. The mythology of virtually every non-desert culture in the world, after all, has used forests as the symbol of choice to denote the supernatural. Woods are, and always have been, soul food for the psyche. Intoxicated by their surroundings, the newcomers to North America, starting with the French, traded woodland images with nearby Indians just as they traded beads for beaver pelts. The immigrants borrowed from hundreds of creation stories, as well as from a mix of mysterious-sounding native spirits, then used them to weave hybrid tales of their own. Native peoples, on the other hand, ended up seasoning their own stories with bits and pieces of Christianity, with European notions about romantic love, and in the case of the northern New England tribes, borrowing entire plots from a series of tales called the "Little Jack Stories," which were first popular in Ireland and France, then changing the heroes into Indians.

In the early nineteenth century poet Rodman Drake penned a wildly popular story called "The Culprit Fay." Like other poets before him he decided to build the tale around the Iroquois belief of Pukwudges—"little vanishers," or "little men of the mountains"—wrapping it in a mix of American forest, Arthurian legend, and ancient Celtic mysticism. In Rodman's poem the little people napped in the trees in cobweb hammocks and hid from the sun under the blooms of four-o'clocks. The minutes of the day were kept by the wood tick. And when it came time for battle, the hero donned an acorn helmet and a shield made from the shell of a ladybug.

A reviewer with the *American Monthly Magazine*, probably being a little generous, called Drake's work one of the most exquisite productions in the English language, rivaled by no poem that had ever appeared on this side of the Atlantic. Drake, he said, had the great good sense to draw his inspiration from the most honorable source a poet could lean on, American nature, studying her up and down until he came to know her "as she lived and breathed in the primal freshness." The result, said the critic, was a fairy tale we could call our own, with imagery that applied to nowhere else under the sun. (There's actually some nifty mystery surrounding this poem. The earliest known spelling of the Iroquois word for these little people was Puck-wud-jees. The "Puck" part of that, which is common to the Algonquian dialect, is in English usually associated with Shakespeare, who used it to denote—what else?—a mischievous spirit, or sprite. It would be amazing to find that Shakespeare picked up the word from early English explorers—they were, after all, interacting with Algonquian tribes thirty years before he died—only to have it resurface again in poems born to his fellow countrymen who came to America.)

In 1845, Drake's poem, along with others by poets such as Henry Wadsworth Longfellow, appeared in a collection called *Forest Legendary*. Long overdue, said reviewers. After all, they argued, it was the forest that was the most American topic of all. Once again, then, there came this notion that it was the art most firmly tied to wild landscape that best spoke to who we were as a people, as a country, which is why the greatest nature and scenery poets in our history—Whitman, Whittier, Bryant, or Emerson—were invariably the same guys who also wrote the most stirring, passionate odes to patriotism.

I'm finding it heartening that so much of western Massachusetts and Connecticut, some of which was still timber-poor even fifty years ago, is again flush with forest—roughly the same number of trees as at the end of the 1700s. And while much of what we have now is a poor man's woods, small trees of the species that even a hungry timber industry tends to scoff at, ravaged by poor management and weakening agents like acid rain, to a people whose lives are spent flying down freeways and hustling through malls and parking garages, even a poor woods can seem awfully good.

Near Cummington, while strolling the grounds of the house where nature-poet William Cullen Bryant was born, I meet a retired teacher in her seventies who tells me that when she was young she could still walk a mile and a half from her home to Lilly Lake across open fields, never having to vary her step to skirt a tree; now that same land is covered in young forest—hemlock, striped maple, beech, yellow birch. "It's beautiful again," she says. "What happened in the eighteen hundreds was that the Ohio Valley lands opened up, and since the soil there was better, people here pulled up stakes and went west. That's when the forest started coming back. The best signs those farms were here at all are the big trees you see. White ash along old driveways. Sugar maples set out next to the house, for maple syrup, or sometimes out in the pasture, as shade for cattle."

Later, while out walking in a nearby woods, I happen to find one of these gargantuan maples, standing at the edge of a shallow bowl laced with beech—probably an old cellar hole. Wrapping my arms around it I can cover no more than a third of its girth; partway through the embrace it occurs to me that whoever used to live here might like it that a hundred and fifty years later, someone happened by and hugged their maple tree.

I remember that when I was living in the Midwest, some

people, mainly farmers, talked as though the return of the woods was a sign of failure, sort of an insult to all the work done by their ancestors to clear and cultivate the land. Personally, I could never see reforestation as a slap at heritage (certainly it was a lesser one than Grandpa's old wood-lot being leveled for a Kmart), but who knows?—maybe those farmers had some old memory resting deep in their bones, genetic fallout from the horrors of the European past. The 1400s for example, when dysentery and typhus and smallpox and plague and measles kept killing people until half the population of northern Europe was either dead or on its way, and great masses of settlers abandoned their farms to make the long trek home to die. And in a very few years, all those places they'd worked so hard to clear and cultivate were under woods again. As if they'd never been.

For my visit to the white pines I've chosen one of the last best second-growth stands in Connecticut—Gold's Stand, which lies unseen and uncelebrated off a tiny road east of West Cornwall. At one time I probably would have opted for the Cathedral Pines, but much of that stand was lost six years ago, sheered off by hurricane winds. At least a dozen people have told me about it, all of them sounding truly sad about the loss, most recently a couple of prep-school kids I pick up hitchhiking to a summer job. "Every kid went there on field trips," one explained. "It was cool. The bus would pull in—everyone'd be goofing off. Then we'd walk into those trees and everybody was like . . . whispering. All of us staring up with our mouths open."

On the fringe of the Gold Stand are hemlock and beech and maple, and in full leaf they form a curtain that hides the heart of the biggest growth, so that when I do finally enter the elder trees it happens all at once, which is kind of shocking. In those few steps there's a shift from the usual woodland America—a tight cluster of mixed hardwood leaves and branches and ground covers dusting my feet—to the woodlands of old: open chambers framed by massive, sky-scraping trunks, each one rising from a clean floor washed in a flood of spent needles.

I find myself seesawing back and forth between seeing this place as a glass half full and one half empty. On one hand, it's awfully fine to lie on my back in the duff and stare up a hundred feet of trunk, imagining specters in green-needled dresses swaying to the summer winds. The bad news is that it's kind of scary to be in a state that can grow trees like lambs grow wool, and have to rummage through the back forty behind the West Cornwall fire station to find a mere couple dozen acres of second growth. Even this stand was nearly lost a number of times: barely saved by dumb luck in the 1870s, when the local railroad decided to start burning coal in its boilers instead of wood; then again seventy years later, narrowly snatched from lumbermen for the sum of five thousand dollars by a remarkably forward-thinking Connecticut General Assembly.

So many woods, so little time. But by the time I walk out from the arms of Gold's white pines, I'm starting to feel the pull of Tennessee. I'm thinking a week down there, maybe two, the urge kindled by nothing more than a small hope of refreshing some of the memories I have as a kid watching those staggering, tree-covered mountains fly by from the road on our way to Florida, and later, in high school, on trips with my brother in his growling, fat-tired Mustang. For sheer variety the forests of the southern Appalachians are among the best on earth. Not that I knew that back then, of course. Then it was just all that wildness hanging in the sweat of summer. It was houses in hollers where people could walk off the front porch into miles of woods—woods with streams and wildflower gardens, black bears and white-tail deer, even mountain lions. What had been the stuff of imagination in northern Indiana was for the first time reality in east Tennessee.

Determined to keep as far away from the freeway as possible I rise at dawn and start moving west through Connecticut on a web of county roads, then begin a long drift south along the Hudson, winding past roadside stands of raspberries and strawberries and honey, past what long ago was a jumble of orchards and hardscrabble farms, much of it now reclaimed by modest runs of woods. To the west the sun is pouring onto the crumpled loaves of the Catskills, turning the Hudson into a breathtaking flash of silver. Unfortunately, a lot of other people are heading south with me, trying to get to work, and the last thing they need is some gawker from Montana driving his van like an old man who just fumbled his glasses out the window. The honk of horns and the occasional dirty look prod me to start searching for a turnoff, and the first one I happen on is a narrow, wooded road leading, according to a sign beside the highway, to a place called "Olana." And so it's quite by accident that I find myself on a high bluff above the Hudson, at the magnificent Persian-style home of that pious nineteenth-century landscape painter, Frederic Church—one of the true geniuses of the Hudson River School, and in the 1850s and 1860s the most famous artist in America. A guy who knew something about woods.

The signs say the museum is closed today, but there are a few employees arriving for work via the back door, so I hang out until Museum Director Jim Ryan arrives, a graceful, articulate man of forty-something, sporting a splendid mustache, who, on hearing of my interest in the forest, is kind enough to invite me inside to glimpse a few of the treasures. Ryan is a fount of knowledge, and when he talks of Frederic Church his voice and the sweep of his arms have the easy comfort of old books and stuffed chairs—the kind of person who leaves you wanting to carry on the conversation in a smoking jacket with a snifter of brandy.

While the outside of the house is a grand splash of Persia, tiles and turrets and braids of spirit-colors, the interior is flat-out cerebral. Nearly every room is filled with art and sacred objects collected from cultures around the world,

China to Assyria to Mexico. As far as Church was concerned this house high above the Hudson overlooked the world's true paradise, this fresh, new Garden of Eden. By filling it with carefully chosen vases and sculptures, tapestries and pottery, he turned it into a shrine, a sanctuary meant to serve as a kind of corrective for all the ills of all the civilizations that had come before—a museum for shards picked up along the path that led finally and inevitably to America. The attention to detail is overwhelming: the quality of the light and the views coming in every window; interior walls wearing paints and designs for which every color was painstakingly mixed on Church's own palettes; the dining table in the so-called "Medieval Room," where the family could eat to soft light pouring through a row of cathedral-style windows, illuminating an enormous run of paintings of various subjects and sizes, some from as far back as the fifteenth century, carefully matched and positioned from low to high, leaving the room looking at first glance as though it's been wallpapered with art.

Because the mansion is closed, there's very little light to guide us, rendering the paintings even more mysterious. In the sitting room is a final sketch for Church's *Cry in the Wilderness*, completed in 1860 and considered by today's scholars the ultimate statement about wilderness in America. A stroll down the walls, viewing such images in murky light, feels like a visit from the Ghost of Christmas Past—one arresting scene after another depicting the deepest, most profound myths, yearnings, and terrors ever to drive our culture. On one wall is a Thomas Cole piece, a dark, disturbing image of the woods, full of the fear that infused early Colonial times. Directly across from it is a solitary lake in New Hampshire, where the forest has been completely transformed. Suddenly the trees are surrounded by light, caressed, wrapped in full-blown, born-again affection. The kind of affection that would for a time come to define the most fully American notion of evil of them all: the thoughtless, grinding destruction of nature. A clue to why, perhaps, seventy years later a guy named Joe Knowles could become famous just by turning his back and walking into the woods.

By the time I make my way back down the drive to the highway—a route Church engineered to make certain every bend offered a perfect glimpse of field or mountain or Hudson River—the southbound rush to work has ended. I settle in again to a happy poking, rolling downstream with the river. Past old German settlements, past the flaky, chalk-colored limestone cliffs towering to the west in the toes of the Catskills. Into Port Jervis, with its neighborhood streets and front porches safely guarded from the heat by the shade of a thousand maple trees; to Milford, birthplace of Gifford Pinchot, the so-called "Father of American forestry," and south farther still, into the narrow fields and wooded ridges of the Delaware Gap, near where Swedish immigrants built America's first log cabin more than three hundred and fifty years ago. Summer has risen to a shout, and the land is thick with buttercups and purple-flowered raspberry, with cinquefoil, butter-and-eggs, clover, Depford pink, and huddles of hay-scented fern. Black and yellow birch lean out over the roadways, shading the edges, and blooms of rhododendron peek through the woods past the hemlock and the white pine.

On past fields in Pennsylvania thick with red clover and woodlots dappled with sumac. Past rows of big, blocky houses in Freeburg and McAlister, their front porches elbowing so close to the highway you can almost reach out and touch them when you pass; and beside the houses, kids on bikes practicing wheelies, and old women in cotton dresses and big straw hats tending thin strips of roses and gladiolas. A parade of radio shows streams in and then fades behind the mountains. In Williamsport, Pennsylvania, a preacher blames society's corruption not on our having abused nature, but on the Beatles, then goes on to warn me that the god of the New Testament is the same one as the god of the Old Testament. "He hasn't grown any older," the preacher says. "He hasn't even learned anything." Later on, in Allegheny County, Maryland, a breathless announcer breaks into the regular broadcast to announce that the Old Town Volunteer Fire Department is on fire.

Past the wooded pockets and hollows of northwest Maryland, down West Virginia through old logging towns where timber companies from Chicago rushed in after the turn of the century and punched railroads up every cranny, cutting nearly every tree. "Used to be a thousand people a week come to square dances in Harmans," says a clerk at a nearby gas station. "Then just like that, it was over." He explains that most of the families were forced out to the cities but that they held on to their property, left it to go to woodlots, turned their noses up at real-estate agents and developers. A lot of them, he says, are still holding on. "There's two kinds of people. Those that came back home, and those that are still hopin' to." It's a story I'll hear told again and again all along the southern Appalachians.

With the invention of the Shay steam locomotive, which could climb steep grades into what were until then inaccessible valleys and hollows, it took less than forty years to wipe out the lion's share of some of the greatest forest systems on earth. Not surprisingly, with the hills denuded there came mud slides and floods without end, a needless, bitter refrain that had already been played out in ancient Greece, in Rome and Venice, in a thousand other times and places around the world. Most of the woodlands I pass today are new arrivals—nurtured by federal protection, such as the magnificent Monongahela National Forest, as well as by Civilian Conservation Corps tree-planting programs in the 1930s.

Of course, when you destroy an ecosystem, you don't necessarily get the same ecosystem the second time around. In West Virginia the astonishing old-growth red spruce groves—the so-called "he-balsam," and probably the finest tree in the world for making the belly of violins—never did manage much of a comeback. Red spruce doesn't reproduce well from stumps, relying instead on sprouts from seed. And the dry, desiccated lands left in the wake of logging made that all but impossible. Instead we got brambles, and then aspen and fire cherry, and finally trees like maple and yellow birch and beech.

The land is turning more southern, the steep hills gone to dogwoods and young Virginia pine, fan-leaved hawthorn and shagbark hickory, locust and crown vetch, ailanthus and moonseed vines. There is so much humidity, so much transpiration from these runs of trees that the hills have grown bleary, weakened from kelly green to murky sage. There's a catchy, spirited prance and gambol to these back roads: From the crest of a ridge you snake down the other side on a ribbon of pavement or dirt that looks like cooked spaghetti tossed on the plate, making your way through beautiful hardwoods and conifers along the way, finally bottoming out into a narrow strip of valley from forty to several hundred yards wide; run that to the far end, then climb up and over another wooded ridge. Over and over again, mile after sweet, twisted mile. The mold is finally broken near Newport, Virginia, in a long and lovely bottom cut through the center by State Highway 42, rimmed by open country, green and gold, much of it dappled with dairy cattle. Signs are up in coffee shops and on yards all along this route, protesting plans for a 750,000-watt power line to be strung down the valley. "APCO Towers," one sign shouts at passerby. "No Need, Just Greed."

Long after passing out of the fight zone, in a town with no traffic lights and a trailer for a post office—a town so small a guy could sneeze on one end and give a cold to somebody on the other—someone has placed a sign with a more universal message: a forty-foot banner hung across the front of a house. "I wouldn't mind the rat race," it says, "if I had more cheese."

Chapter Six

Lester and Darla Simpson live at the poor end of Stevens Holler. The high side, up-country, past where the road gets so skinny you can't drive without your bumpers kissing walls of mint and pokeberry, where the land is wrinkled and steep, tossed like salad, covered with woods. A couple of miles down the road is the Wilbert place, and while it's true that old Roy Wilbert has to make a sharp climb to get from his mailbox back to the front porch of his house—no small feat for someone ninety-five, even if he is a faith healer—once up there, he's at least got a terrace close to flat enough to be worked without rolling the tractor. Farther down still is the Widow Johnson place, flat enough even for a good half-acre of lawn, which seventy-five-year-old Alice keeps in good order by pushing a power mower across it once a week. And by the time you reach the mouth of the holler, things get downright level, broad and well-watered enough to grow respectable patches of tobacco and field corn, and long sweeps of juicy melons.

But not here. Not at the end of this long dirt driveway barely holding its own against the weeds, next to a root cellar that Lester helped his daddy build some twenty years ago, and an old barn that has posts leaning up against the outer walls to keep it from falling down. The house is small, maybe four hundred square feet, with tar-paper walls and a tin roof, a single-seat outhouse squatting out back in a patch of wild mint. There's no sign of anyone stirring, so I grab my notebook and tape recorder and head for the front door, passing a porch rail lined with faded, freshly washed jeans, and bundles of catnip, each neatly tied and hung in a line to cure. It's dark past the screen door but I can make out the sound of a TV turned low—theme music of some kind—and then an announcer welcoming viewers back to the *700 Club*. I mean only to give a modest knock but the door is loose in the frame and when I hit it, it makes a terrible rattle, and I'm standing here wishing I could take it back. Finally a couple comes to the door, each around thirty, hair matted, looking sleepy. Lester has on a pair of worn jeans and a thin, white-cotton T-shirt that stretches like a second skin over his muscled shoulders and slight paunch. His face resembles a kid's face, smooth and round, but his eyes have a touch of hardness, making the kid part seem a little bit bully. Darla, on the other hand, though barely five feet tall is lean and strong, dark-skinned with a sharp chin and nightfall eyes, and long, straight hair that hangs to the lower part of her back—her grandpa's look, she likes to say—Cherokee blood.

Given that Lester is a moonshiner I waste no time identifying myself, offering the name of the local woman who suggested I look them up, explaining how I've come from Montana to learn about the woods. Darla's quick to offer a smile—seems she's already heard through the grapevine I'd be coming—invites me in, shows me to a green, threadbare couch, its cushions squished into bucket seats. The walls of the living room are made of uncoated pressboard, empty but for a few taped-up pictures of flowers, and one of a doe and two fawns grazing in a meadow. The roof has leaks in it, leaving places where the upper walls and ceiling have warped into waves, sprouting mushroom- and teardrop-shaped stains; it's a weather record of sorts, fingerprints left by some of east Tennessee's more rollicking mountain thunderstorms. The old saw flashes through my head about the woman who asks her husband when he plans to fix the roof: "Can't work up there when it's raining," he tells her. "And when it's not, well, there isn't any need."

Darla turns off the sound from the *700 Club* but leaves the picture, then sits down at the other end of the couch. Lester settles into the single stuffed chair, watches me fumbling with my notebook, then reaches over and takes a .45 pistol from the top of the end table. He turns it in his hand a few times, angling it so the blue steel of the barrel catches the light coming off Pat Robertson's forehead. Now and then it comes to rest pointing at me, hangs there for a minute, then twirls off around the room again. When Darla sees this, she shifts so her whole body is turned toward her husband. I'm imagining—hoping would be a better way to put it—that she's angling to give him a dirty look or a shake of the head or something of the sort, anything to discourage him. After what seems like a long time, she draws him in for a couple of seconds, then he breaks back toward me. "Just so you're who you say you are," he says to me, being as friendly as a man can be in such an awkward moment. "Cause if you're not—Ya know some of the boys 'round here find people snooping around where they oughtn't be, they just rough them up. But the way I figure, by then the damage is done."

One of Lester's relatives I met a couple days ago called him "a colorful boy"; another, more candid, said that for a long time Lester himself preferred the term "holy terror, crazy motherfucker of the Holler." Some say he settled down when he met Darla, that she was just the right mix of smart and tough, and give him credit for knowing a good woman when she came along. One old man said it might also have had something to do with an incident years back, on a winter night when some of the neighbors caught him stealing and as punishment, roughed him up, stripped him naked and tied him with ropes, threw him in the back of a pickup and sped up and down the country roads till daybreak, when they dumped him back on his front lawn, bruised butt, numb nuts and all. "Whatever you do in your early life," Lester will tell me later, "in this hollow, that's what you are forever. If you're a drug addict for five years and then go straight, you're always a drug addict."

I press on, uncap my pen, ask Lester what it was like to grow up here, make a couple of meaningless scrawls in my notebook, trying to look like a writer and not a fed. He keeps the gun in his hand for another minute, then, content he's made his point, sets it down again, gently, like it was something alive. "There's thirteen in my family," he says. "Twelve livin' and one dead. We grew up right here. My daddy farmed this land, right where you're sittin', with a mule and a plow. These little fields you see, that's what he made his livin' on. Growed tobacco, growed corn and peas and potatoes—whatever you could put in a jar and set back there in that can house."

Darla nods, probably eager to keep things rolling, but also, I think, taken by the images, as if they could have come from her own life. "Tell him 'bout the woods," she says. Then to me: "That's what you said you was writin' about, isn't it?"

Lester takes a deep breath. "Well, I don't know. Dad got diabetes somewhere along the way, and after that, 'bout the only meat we ever ate came from these woods. I 'member one winter—maybe I was nine or ten—all we had was soup beans. So I busted the neighbor's wood for him and he'd trade me shells for it. Then I'd go out and shoot squirrels or rabbits or coons and that's what we ate. You could sell 'possum hides for around four 'n' a half dollars, and with that money we'd buy coffee and sugar."

"There was plants, too," Darla adds. "There's always people wantin' to buy things like sang [ginseng] and pennyroyal and lobelia. You could go out there right now and collect herbs for money, but you'd have to be good at knowin' where to look. My granddaddy was Cherokee, a medicine man, and my daddy was a healer, so I learned way back how to find all that stuff. Right now sang is sellin' for forty dollars a pound."

Lester scratches his chin, smiling at something. "Moss," he finally says. "When I was a kid, seven or eight maybe, Hugh Bible was buying this moss, then he'd take it over to Rome Mountain and sell it. Used it to make floral arrangements, I think. Had to be log moss, now, with a bark back. When I first started pullin' it, it was sellin' for eighteen cents a pound."

He goes on for another thirty minutes, describing early teen years spent wielding chain saws with his older brother—cutting hardwood, or knocking down jack-pine stands and rolling the trees down the hills to the road. "Then we'd send one of our sisters to walk back for the truck—five or ten miles sometimes—load it up and drive it on down to the mill."

Sitting listening to all this, I can't help but compare my own work life at that age, which consisted mostly of roaming the neighborhood looking for lawns to mow. The more he talks, the clearer it becomes just how well Lester understands the workings of these woods, the mechanics of the place. While he can't read or write, he knows a lot about plant succession—when the first flush of pokeberry and raspberry will show up after a clear-cut, how long until the birch and aspen suckers start to rise. Beyond that he knows how each of those stages affects birds and animals—which ones prosper, and when, and which ones lose out. The kind of knowledge based on where to go for dinner on the table or money for gas in the car or to pay the doctor bill. Learning ecology in order to have a better shot at a pot of 'possum stew.

"Ya know, speakin' of loggin', it's good to keep an eye on those clear-cutters," Lester is saying. "Sometimes the bastards don't know when to quit. Where they've really screwed us is with the water. So much of it polluted. When I was a kid rivers were black as tea. People run their dogs in the Pigeon to get rid of the mange. Have athlete's foot or somethin' like that, the river's where you'd go. Just eat it right off."

Such flinching over timber-company practices is more common in these parts than I ever expected; the old men especially seem to have no use at all for big clear-cuts, almost as if they're suffering hangovers from the pillage they saw in the 1940s. "Don't have much time left," Henry, seventy-nine, told me outside the grocery store. "Just wanna enjoy it like it is."

Who knows?—Maybe there's even a little lingering resentment over trampling the forest lore of their Scotch, Irish, and English ancestors. Many fathers of today's old men, for example, were very much of a mind to spare some of the bigger oaks they came across while out cutting timber, because such trees were thought to be special. Best thing you could do for the really big ones, people said, was to let them live out their allotted time. Around the turn of the century a man named Lorane Cash was out scouting trees near here for roofing material, and ended up felling a big walnut. Inside, toward the heart of the tree, he found a coil of black human hair, buried a good foot from the bark. Likely it was from the days when people thought you could cure certain diseases by boring a hole in a tree (often an oak), placing a clip of hair from the crown of your head inside and sealing it with a wooden plug. By the time the tree grows over the plug, the saying went, the disease will have disappeared.

That gun lying on the end table in easy reach makes me slow to ask about other uses of the woods, like moonshining, but I'm going to bring it up sometime and now seems as good as any. "This isn't something you have to answer if you don't want to," I tell Lester, as if he didn't already have a pretty good understanding of that. "But I'd sure like to learn a little about the moonshine business. Kind of seems hard to talk about life in the woods without it." For a minute, he doesn't say anything. Then again, neither does he reach for the gun. Finally he takes a breath and crosses his legs, leans back in that old stuffed chair, like he's settling in for a long story.

"I was about ten. Somethin' like that. My daddy had this old shotgun—hell, that thing kicked hard. So one day I take it and tell Mama I'm going hunting, but instead I go out to one of these stills I know about. There were two men there working it—course I knew who they were. Well, I wanted some of that moonshine to sell, and they agreed to that, but not before warning me that I'd damn sure better not be plannin' on stealin' it. And that's how it started. For five dollars I'd buy half-gallon jars of pot liquor, wrap 'em in burlap, then carry 'em off the mountain on my back, one or two at a time. Later, I'd break 'em down into half pints and sell those for three dollars apiece. Some to friends. Most of it to the local store."

Lester made thirty to fifty dollars a week right from the start, but he says that in order to cover his tracks, he also helped out on local farms, earning seventy-five cents an hour. Later he worked with one of his relatives who had a still, pushing a wheelbarrow three miles through the woods—sugar going in, pot liquor coming out. No surprise he was the first of his age to buy a car—a 1966 Plymouth Fury—though a few weeks later he got to drinking the product, wrecked the Fury at the top of Bell Mountain. "Had a brand-new battery in it, so I pulled it out and carried it all the way back down that mountain." His next rig was a '46 International, with rails on the bed, which he used to start bootlegging for real. "Makin' five hundred a week and not killin' myself. Hell. You can believe this or not, but for a while my main supplier was a sheriff. Was a time that feller had a dozen stills goin' at once."

Lester is remarkably patient with my questions, and I've got a lot of them. In fact, it strikes me he's awfully concerned I get this right. "Where you set up a still in the woods has to do with the water—you've got to taste it careful and make sure it's good for makin' liquor. I'll tell you now there are dirty moonshiners out there. You know what that is? No? Well, it's doin' things like dumpin' old car batteries in to make the mash work off faster. You can make moonshine four times as fast doing that, turnin' it in a couple days instead of two weeks, but that's the shit that makes people go blind. I even know guys who put their wives' dirty panties in—you know, they think the yeast will help. Another trick goes on all the time is to use baby oil; some add that to make the stuff bead, same as it would with a high alcohol content. Good moonshine looks like teardrops slidin' down the glass."

Just outside is the sound of a car door slamming shut. Images of ATF agents are flashing through my head, though I'm imagining them as guys with fedoras and tommy guns, like Elliot Ness and The Untouchables. "Must be the day for company," Darla says, and I follow a couple of paces behind them out to the porch for a look. Walking toward us in the distance is a three-hundred-pound man in a black Harley-Davidson T-shirt, barefoot, moving at the pace of a mud turtle, picking every step as if the driveway were lined with glass. His beard is neatly trimmed, leaving him looking like Pavarotti gone off to join the Hell's Angels.

"Where's your shoes, Jim?" Lester yells out, but Jim's too busy scowling to reply. "Jim was in Vietnam," Lester tells me in a low voice. "His legs are all fucked up." By the time he reaches the porch Jim seems near collapse, and Darla, thoroughly dwarfed by the guy, takes his arm and ushers him into the living room, where he settles onto the old green couch. "This here's Gary," Lester tells him. "He's writin' a book on the woods."

"Most beautiful woods in the world," says Jim. "And I've seen a lot of the world."

He tells Lester the Jehovah's Witnesses came by his place again last week, that this time it was three big guys, and he and Lester start laughing like hell. Darla rolls her eyes. Lester sees my confused look and jumps in to explain. Seems a month ago he was sitting out on his porch pulling on a big joint when a guy and two women from Jehovah's Witness came up to do a little proselytizing, which took a bit of courage, considering Lester was sitting there buck-naked. Well, they didn't get twenty words out before Lester stands up, claims to be the devil himself, then lets it be known he's looking for a woman to carry his wild child. At which point the Witnesses apologize for the interruption, make a hasty retreat, head on down the road toward Lester's Aunt Sally's house. Inspired by his success, Lester heads off through the woods at full clip, sneaks in the back of Sally's place and opens the front door, wearing only that big grin on his face, right as the Witnesses are walking onto the front porch. "Haven't seen 'em in this holler since," Lester says proudly, like it was community service in capital letters.

The four of us make small talk for a while. Suddenly Darla catches a sign from Lester, gets up and asks me if I'd like to go out with her to see some of the herbs they use for doctorin'. Lester and Jim, it would appear, have a little business to tend to. Outside, Darla talks of being fourteen and not being able to wait until school was out so she could run to the woods.

"I'd find a few wild apples or somethin' to eat and then climb up in a birch tree and stay there for hours, sometimes past dinner. And when I got thirsty, I knew where every good spring was to get a drink. Mama worried about me sometimes, but that was just me."

Darla is one of five daughters, all but one brought into this world by the hand of a rather celebrated midwife of the hollers, known as Granny Nichols. She's both amazed and saddened by the women friends she's made over the past few years who have absolutely no hands-on knowledge of the woods—says most of them don't have a clue to what to gather when their kids have a cold or the flu, that some have never even picked poke salad greens for dinner. It's a mystery to her why someone would be willing to live with such a handicap.

"This here's catnip," she says, proudly fingering the leaves from a huge bundle hanging on the porch wall. "Now before doctors' medicine come out, it was used for babies. Like a baby had the fever or the hives or somethin', they'd boil this tea. Then they'd take and sweeten it and give it to the baby just as hot as it could be drunk. As soon as he drank the last drop of tea, they'd put that baby to bed, and it would sweat that fever out. Shoot, if I have the flu or somethin' I'll boil up a patch of it—I've often sat here before goin' to bed and drunk half a gallon. And it'll make you sleep—it's about like taking sleeping pills. Won't have no crazy dreams or nothin'."

As we walk along, what I saw on my way in as patches of weeds now turn into pharmacies. Yellow root for ulcers and goldenseal for mouth sores. Mint for sore muscles and gas pains. Lobelia for asthma and coughs, pennyroyal to induce menstruation and as an insect repellent. "This here's rattlesnake master," Darla says. "Say an animal gets snake-bit, dig that root up and mash it up, and put it in something it'll eat. When he eats it, it'll run that poison right out of 'im. Uh, you might wanna watch where you're walkin'," she says, pointing right at my feet. "Lots of copperheads right there."

She says if I really want to learn about how to use the plants of the woods, I should find one of the last of the old Cherokee medicine men still living up in the hills over toward North Carolina. "They's the only ones left that still know the old ways," she says sadly. "You'd need lots of time, though—there's just a few, and it's tough to get them to talk. Ya can't come right out and ask because as likely as not they'll say they don't know what you mean. After a while, though, could be they'd come around."

When I get ready to leave Lester tells me I really need to meet up with him again tonight, and we'll go over to this local whorehouse, see Brenda, and man, Brenda will do things us Montana boys have never even thought about. "It's kinda rough," he admits, "but you stick close by me and you'll be fine," and he pats the gun beside his chair. It's nice of him to offer and all, and I'm sure it'd be the trip of a lifetime, but in truth about the last place in the world I want to end up is in a whorehouse in a dry county, trying to watch my backside, with Lester hovering somewhere nearby slamming down moonshine. I tell him I'm planning to be out on the trail tonight, which is true, and he gives me this sad, thoughtful stare, a look of pity, really, as if he's thinking that as wonderful as the woods are, it's a lost man who'd choose them over Brenda.

America's woods have long been harbor to people who come in shapes that don't quite fit in the square, measured holes the rest of us have wangled our lives into. People used to say that was one of the true blessings of the frontier forest—that it had places like army forts and logging camps, where ruffians could go to work off a little of the vinegar that so irritated the rest of society. And while there's no more frontier, clearly there are still wind-blasted, chalky barrens in the Southwest fit to cradle a few thousand desert rats, patches of woods in the Rockies and Midwest and South for the boys who like to play with guns, and in the Appalachians, secluded hollers that can keep more secrets than even people like Lester can spin out in the course of a lifetime.

I'm spending nights alone in the woods on Round Mountain, just west of the high, wooded border of east Tennessee and North Carolina, in the heart of the southern Appalachians. Rain has been falling off and on for the past twenty-four hours; I can hear each wave approach as drops battering the distant leaf canopy, then running toward camp across the forest on the tops of the yellow birch and hemlock and American chestnut—falling on the whorls of umbrella magnolia, on tulip trees and witch hazel and sweet gum. At times it seems like the upper branches of the trees are all that keep the clouds from swallowing up the world. Yet for all the moisture, the country holds it well. The water seeps into six inches of dead leaves, down to bathe the roots, finally into the water table, giving rise to countless creeks and springs. Instead of my usual wake-up ritual of sticking my head in a creek, this morning I strip down to a pair of shorts and stand out on the top of the picnic table in the pouring rain—face to the sky, arms outstretched, pausing every so often to slake sheets of cool water from my hair and arms and legs.

Most of the trees near my camp are middle-aged, the canopies of the largest towering some sixty to eighty feet above the mountain, the lion's share of the stand open enough to wander through at will. The trunks wear patchy, threadbare coats of lichen the color of olives and chalk, and along the streams the ground is wrapped in cushions of moss—the kind hunters used to stuff into cotton sacks for pillows. The air smells like ginger and pepper and bags of peat. After three days I still can't get over the profusion of life on these ridge tops, in this jumble of hollows and stream cuts and glades. Here almost every month is wrapped in some new leaf or blossom, the blush of plants striking the passing of the year as surely as a clock chimes the hours of a day. Spring beauty in February. Sourwood and mountain myrtle in June. August with its bee balm and monkshood and turtlehead. Witch hazel from November through January.

At the moment, though, best of all are the rhododendron, still in full bloom. Now that the catawba and dogwood have come and gone, this is the last truly outrageous flower of the season. At the end of the day, long after the rest of the woods has grown dark and murky, these cream-and-cerise blooms are still visible—glowing on the hillsides and ridge lines like nightlights. They coax imagination down the hills and into their tangled thickets, into the kind of woody knots that have been favorite hiding places for moonshiners in Appalachia for some two hundred years. "You best be careful snooping around in those woods," said Charlotte, the beautician at Helen's Hair Fashions in Newport. "That goes double if you've got out-of-state plates."

Early in the afternoon the clouds break and the rain gives up. I grab my day pack, toss in some bread and cheese, amble off up the Appalachian Trail through woodland gardens of strawberry, withe rod, jewelweed, heal all, blackberries, and the scarlet blush of bee balm. Beyond Lemon Gap are places where the path tunnels through massive, ten-foot-high thickets of rhododendron, some of which are losing their blossoms, leaving me to walk through the arbors on a thin film of ivory petals. Even better are the countless chestnut stumps—enormous granddaddy trees that were long ago victims of chestnut blight, then later of the ax and saw, yet even today refuse to give themselves up to the soil. Willy Walker's grandfather, ninety-seven now, tells of there being so many chestnuts in the fall they'd roll down the hills and pile against logs and into small slumps in the ground, leaving him to collect them with a grain scoop. Some of the older men in Del Rio have told me of cutting these giants back in the thirties, after the blight hit, using two-man crosscut saws—felling them, slicing them into sixteen-foot lengths, then dragging them with teams of horses down to the road to load onto big flatbed trucks. "You could never fit but three of 'em on a trailer," Jess explained. "That's how big they was."

Of course the loss of chestnuts left the American woods poorer from an aesthetic sense, wiping out much of that trollish, druidscape feel. But more important to the people in these hollers was that the death of the chestnut trees meant the loss of an important part of their subsistence. For one thing, during the Depression most people around here boiled and baked, sliced and diced chestnuts every day and every way to round out their meals. Even worse was that in losing these groves, families could no longer turn out their pigs and let them fatten on chestnuts and then collect them for slaughter in the fall. After the blight, hogs were kept only by those few people lucky enough to be able to feed them, leaving more empty space on the dinner plates than ever before.

After some five miles I arrive on a treeless, broad-shouldered upland draped in a summer shawl of red clover, buttercups, highbush blueberry, butter-and-eggs, and great sweeps of yarrow. "Max Patch," they call this place. Once a chestnut forest, cut out and turned into a sheep ranch, now an extraordinary, wind-blasted summit from which the world falls away to the east in wave after wave of timber disappearing into a distant haze. Hopewell Ridge and Betsy Gap and Dogged Knob, Farmer Mountain and Little Sandy Mush Bald. Settled-looking mountains, all soft shoulders and melted meringue, cut here and there by bowls and hollows filled with trees, sunlit and sweating like so many terrariums, giving rise to an incredible variety of plants, some found nowhere else in the world. A tenacious, mysterious run of country, much of it just sixty or seventy years from the saw and already full of life, full of texture.

The show ends fast when a steel-colored sheet of cloud comes out of the woods to the west at a fast walk and begins drawing over the Patch. As it crosses the far side, it turns sharply downward, hugging the steep slope—first in tattered shreds, then swelling to a heavy blanket—until I'm standing beside an enormous river and waterfall of clouds pouring off the edge of the Patch and down the side of the mountain. Minutes later it's completely engulfed me, but for one small, pie-shaped window through which I can see a lone farmhouse miles away in a distant bottom, lit by a full shaft of sunlight, and then that too is gone.

Where five minutes earlier I could look into next week, now I can barely see the moment; visibility is down to two hundred feet, then one hundred, then fifty. I can smell the moisture as it breaks across my face. One last time the clouds rip open to reveal a sunlit grove of oak trees far below, and then all goes gray for good. Nothing now but a tiny, bleak patch of grass and wildflowers robbed of their color. It's all I can do to find the main trail again and make my way back into the woods—back along those stretches of trail strewn with rhododendron blossoms, past the chestnut stumps too big for two people to put their arms around, back to Round Mountain.

Time in the big woods is marked not so much by where the sun hangs in the sky as by the cast of shadows, by which layers of the canopy are lit, by the sound of afternoon thunder and the stir of leaves when warm valley air rushes up the sides of the mountains. Night fades to day and day to night with less fanfare here, and yet when darkness does come, it's absolute.

Back at camp, late in the evening, folksinger Stan Rogers comes on the radio, live from Halifax, Nova Scotia, so I grab my harmonica, sprawl out on the floor of the van, and play out a couple of tunes with him while the wind tosses a few raindrops through the open door. Even though full darkness is just a breath away, the rhododendron blossoms are still visible. Pretty soon the lightning bugs start cruising, thousands of them, running through the dark past the rhododendron blossoms, like tiny space ships shuttling back and forth between a cluster of pale moons.

Gene, at the grocery store in Del Rio, has told me I should stop in and visit with Henry Johnson—"a fella who knows these woods"—so in the morning between hikes I call his house, talk to his wife, and she tells me to come by in the evening, about dark, when Henry gets in from the fields. He's a brawny farmer with a thick, muscled chest and shoulders, and hands as big as the melons he grows. But despite his size, there's an easy grace to his movements, like someone who just got off the dance floor after a long waltz and hasn't quite given up the music. His shirt and coveralls hang loose, worn and smudged from another long day in the melon fields, but his face is among the calmest I've seen—bright, rested eyes, wrinkled at the corners, pooled above a thick white beard—kind of a Kenny Rogers meets Moses. We sit in old stuffed chairs in the basement of a simple house, piles of laundry around us, arrowheads plucked from the fields, then fastened to boards and hung on the cinderblock walls, and here and there, beautiful handmade quilts.

At first, Henry sits askew from me, turning his head sideways to make eye contact. But as the night goes on—as we get deeper into our talk of the woods—his body adjusts until he's on the edge of the worn cushion of his chair, facing full into the conversation, recalling tales of Grandpa building log barns by ax and of finding sang roots the size of his massive thumbs; of being a kid helping his daddy strip bark from chestnut oaks and cart it down to the road, where it was loaded into trucks and taken to the leather tannery in Newport.

In time, Henry's wife Betty joins us, a round, shy woman, as well as their son John, and before long it seems like a family huddle, full of great conversation about going to the woods and coming back with blackberries for jam, huckleberries to serve up with dumplings. "Oh, ya have-ta try that," Mrs. Johnson tells me soberly—about the virtues of pennyroyal tea.

When I finally get up to leave around eleven, Mrs. Johnson hands me three buckeyes—"They'll bring you luck," she says—and then Henry and John follow me out to the van, stopping first at the back of a pickup truck loaded with melons to offer me two massive Superstar cantaloupes. The moon is nearly full, and clouds skate across the face of it like ghosts dancing; the air is warm and sticky, sweet with the smell of earth. We shake hands again, agree to meet up the holler on Saturday night at Hillbilly's—"a real experience if you're kin to music," they assure me—and then I'm gone, driving again, back up the twisted road through the thick hardwood forests of Round Mountain.

When I reach the campground, the first thing I do is grab a knife and one of those melons, haul them out to the picnic table and slice the fruit open. It's sharp and sweet and when I take a bite the juice fills my mouth, runs down my chin, and I don't stop until I've excavated the entire half down to the thin, bitter green of the rind. I cover the other half with some plastic wrap and slip it in the cooler—breakfast for tomorrow—crawl into bed, fall asleep to the sound of nothing at all.

Chapter Seven

If I hadn't already lost my heart to the woods of east Tennessee, I would have lost it again tonight, Saturday, at the end of a long drive on a web of dirt roads, hopscotching past hand-painted signs with big blue arrows pointing me ever on to the foot of Laurel Mountain, and Hillbilly's. I park on the grass, along with at least fifty or sixty other cars, walk across a patch of open ground below a modest house wrapped in tar paper and to the base of a grand run of forest, to some hundred and fifty folding chairs set up in the open air, facing a small wooden stage where six musicians who live nearby—five from the same family—are plucking and singing great licks of bluegrass, every now and then someone climbing up from the audience to belt out a song or two about some lost darlin' or a homesick tale about missing the sweet hills of Tennessee. Between the stage and the chairs, eighty-year-old men in overalls and six-year-old kids, middle-aged women in cotton dresses, and teenagers too, are all crowded together, spilling out a hearty mix of buck dancing and flat foot, every kick sending tiny clouds of cornmeal and grits flying up from the wooden floor. Nearby is a food stand with hamburgers and hot dogs—Betty Johnson is back there running the grill—as well as fried pies, moon pies, and ice cream. Behind the concessions are two plywood outhouses, each with a hillbilly of the appropriate sex painted on the door.

The name "Hillbilly" was for years the CB handle of Paul Stinson, the owner and creator of this special brand of good time. Paul tells me it all got started several years ago, when God took him up on a promise Paul had made to turn his life around if only the Lord would deliver him from a terrible six-month stint in the hospital, battered by chronic lung disease and the effects of a serious drinking problem . . . if only He'd let him sit on this tiny porch for one more year just to look at Laurel Mountain. That was six years ago. God kept His part of the bargain, and sure enough, Paul did too, building this stage as a place for his neighbors to come have some good clean fun on Saturday nights. There's no booze here, of course, and during the five hours I'm here, I spot only two guys swigging out of a jar off in the shadows of the parking lot, being incredibly secretive about it, knowing full well that Paul would kick them out if he saw it.

After being drug out to the dance floor several times and making it clear to just about everyone how not to go about buck dancing, I hide out in the shadows for a while to catch my breath. Arlis is next to me, a thin, seventy-something man who moved away from these hollers to Cleveland some thirty-five years ago to find work, but like about everyone else who did the same thing, still comes back every chance he gets. "I just feel more at home down here," he admits. "People here, they got thick bark." In his younger days Arlis was a woodcutter. Far from being wistful about it, though, he recalls the time with a look on his face like someone who just swallowed a June bug, going on about how his daddy put him to the crosscut saw when he was just ten years old and then worked him every damn day until he dropped. He hated it so much that at fifteen he ran away from home, lied about his age to get into the army, didn't come back for three years.

After a time, Frank joins us, another old cutter from way back, and before long the two of them are telling me about the finer points of sawing. "The balance is the thing," Arlis is saying. "It's a rocking motion, and the guy dragging the blade back has to be willing to pull up, and then push down as he moves it forward again. If you don't lift up when you're dragging back, it damn near kills the guy you're sawin' with." Of course, they say, as tough as it was, the saw is nothing next to working all day with an ax. Over the course of an hour I hear plenty more: how often you need to sharpen a saw if you're cutting oak or hickory as opposed to white pine or poplar (twice a day versus once every two days); that hitting a hemlock knot is like trying to saw through glass; about how the military guys came into these hills during the war and marked all the big yellow poplars they could find, then hired the men to cut them so they could turn them into props for airplanes. And finally, how it takes two people to drink moonshine—one holds a shotgun to your head to get you to take a drink, and then you trade off.

The truth is, the only thing as good as the music and the dancing are the stories, enough to fill up a whole holler. Stories about moonshine and Granny Nichols, about running away from home, even about church. "The more churches ya have," says one old-timer, "the more split apart people get. The less they stand together. You grow a little marijuana or make some moonshine here in these woods, somebody turns you in, it's always somebody from another church. No gettin' on together."

That talk, in turn, leads someone else to mention Roy Wilbert, a faith healer I sat with for part of an afternoon talking about God, right after finishing my lessons with Lester Simpson about making moonshine. "Funny thing about Roy," George is telling me. "Friend of mine was over to his place helpin' out with some chores, and Roy was there, out in the yard, sayin' his mornin' prayers. He was loud about it—it wasn't like my friend was listenin' on purpose, understand. Anyway, somebody had given Roy a bunch of turkeys, and they'd caught somethin' and were dying off right and left. So Roy's prayin' his thank-yous to the Lord, sayin' how grateful he was for all His blessings. 'You've given me so much, God,' he's a sayin', all proper like. 'This fine life and this here house and family, and I do so thank You. You blessed me with these turkeys, too. Course You should know they weren't worth a damn, they's all dyin' off faster than I can count.' "

Farmers and implement salesmen and housewives and old railroad men; grocers and attorneys and professors, even a mailman. Shy kids and fat kids, little girls in dresses with their hair tied in bows, great grandmas and grandpas, all here tonight, all at home. I've seen family reunions with a lot less of the familiar. Among the crowd there're several Vietnam veterans, including one of the band members, who with thirty-five fellow paratroopers jumped smack into a minefield. Says he got torn up awfully bad but at least ended up living to tell about it—the only one of twelve to survive. Another man is in a wheelchair, paralyzed in the same war, neighbor to a couple I'm spending the night with. "Don't be surprised if you hear shooting across the road around dawn," they'll tell me later. Jerry's fond of his target practice.

So many shot-up, banged-up vets in these hollers, so many men counting on the solitude of these wooded hills.

There's one more person I've been wanting to meet before leaving east Tennessee, and finally, about the time I'm thinking it won't happen, I get my chance. John Bishop and I are sitting outside his home high on a hill, side by side in lawn chairs, on a deck that seems to be floating in the trees. From here most of the world lies downhill, across a crumpled mix of wooded dips and holes and ravines, all clad either in creeping shadows or the kind of late-afternoon light that looks like it's been run through a smear of honey. A scarlet tanager lets out blurry warbles from the branch of a nearby oak. A stone's throw to the east, in the next holler, is where some seventy years ago a young teacher by the name of Catherine Marshall came to teach the children of the hill folk—an encounter Hollywood resurrected a couple of years ago in a television movie called *Christy*. Some of the old-timers around here still seem offended at how the studio depicted kids in that show: soiled and smudged. "Mind now," as one woman told me, clearly upset, "it never did cost us nothin' for soap."

The last time young Americans were overcome by the rosy notion of moving back to the land was in the late 1960s and early 1970s. More than a few, like John Bishop, ended up right here in these green, long-forgotten hills of North Carolina and Tennessee. Bishop had a Ph.D. in physiological psychology from Berkeley under his belt, and had already tucked away a banner year of post-doctoral work at Yale, studying monkeys and cats to map how behavioral response patterns are organized in the brain. The long and short of it was that although he was awfully good at that, it wasn't giving him much satisfaction. One night a friend caught his ear and filled it with her own special brand of sweet tales from the road, of recent wanderings and adventures in Morocco and southern Europe. Not long afterward, to the complete shock and dismay of his colleagues at Yale, Bishop bade farewell to the hallowed halls and set off for rural Spain.

"There were hordes of people on the road then," he says, looking a little homesick at the memory of it. "Travelers from all over the world. I rented a farm for a year, raised a big garden, felt like a king. There was a strong sense of local culture there. We learned from the peasants how to adapt to the place. I got a glimpse of what a self-sustained local community might feel like, and I liked it. I decided that was how I wanted to live."

So on returning to the United States in 1971, Bishop hit the road on a quest for a piece of land. Forest, he was thinking. One that might give him some of the flush he'd had as a kid growing up in the woods of northeast Connecticut. They started in California, he and a woman companion, but it was way too expensive. From there to Arizona and New Mexico, where he says bad feelings between the hippies and the locals were running high. Then on to Arkansas, and finally here to east Tennessee. "I can't tell you how right this place felt," he adds, leaning forward in the chair to catch my eye. "Some of it had to do with the fact that there was a long-established culture here. It's changed a lot now, but even twenty years ago, people were still farming with mules, still growing most of their own food. Nearly everyone got life from this forest—they were related to it, familiar with every part of it."

"But those tensions you found in New Mexico and Arizona," I say. "The stress between the locals and the hippies. That didn't happen here?"

"It wasn't like that at all. The old-timers got a kick out of the idea of these rich kids with educations coming here, throwing the big life aside and coming to a place like this. I'm sure they thought we were kind of crazy—predicted most of us wouldn't last, and they were right. But they were always warm to us, supportive. Even now, a total stranger, they'll invite you into the house, serve you a meal, ask you to spend the night. Everybody I knew back in those early days had some local contact or neighbor down the road that was a fount of helpful information."

When his daughter had a nasty planter's wart, it was Darla Simpson' daddy, the healer, who cured it—put his hand on it, Bishop recalls, offered some kind of incantation, told her it would disappear in a couple of days, and it did. It was Granny Nichols who midwifed the birth of his son, who's turning eighteen this year.

"It was a tough birth," he says, sighing, shaking his head at the memory. "Eight hours of labor from the time his head first appeared. All night long Granny worked the birth canal and I pushed, carefully, right where she told me to. Slowly, together we worked him out. When it was over, my wife was so wrecked I had to turn her over in bed—she couldn't move. That was about eight in the morning, and I remember Granny going out and fixing this big breakfast for everybody—for me, her family, maybe six or seven other women who were there about to give birth. Then she went out and did her regular chores, like nothing had happened. Charged us fifteen dollars. It was always fifteen dollars, whether you were there for a day or a week."

John is as loyal to his mountain-folk neighbors as anyone I've met—humbled by their talents, inspired by their willingness to give. Yet some twenty-five years ago, Bishop gave something to them—something in truth he'd rather forget about, but that some of them prize like few other things plucked from the world at large.

Late last night, just before I left Hillbilly's, four old men stood in a half-circle, hands in their coveralls, telling me about having to leave these woods in the 1940s and early 1950s, how they and their friends went north to Cincinnati and Detroit, Cleveland and Indianapolis, taking jobs in factories because the woods were plundered and there was no work in Appalachia. Just in describing those years, they wore the kind of suffering, downcast looks most of us might reserve for talking about a long hitch in prison. It wasn't that they were country bumpkins afraid of the big city, afraid of change, but more that they had an honest-to-God ache for this place, a yearning for home and family that ran so bone-deep it nearly crippled them. In listening to them I found myself envious, wishing I could love a place that much. Some of them finally made it back, and of those, several concluded what their kin had decided decades before, during the Depression: that they'd do what they had to do to stay on this land. And if that meant a slice of the outlaw life, then so be it.

By the time John Bishop arrived, people had been growing marijuana in these woods for years. But it was a primitive effort: Set out a bunch of plants in spring, whack them down in August and bale them like so much hay, toss everything into a bag and sell it for ten or twenty bucks a pound. But Bishop came from California, where pot was tended like the royal tea roses. During his first couple of years in the hollers he shared some of that knowledge, discreetly, with two or three locals. Pretty soon an awful lot of people—some young, some well into their nineties—were growing better and better pot, hiding it in east-west slashes in the forest.

Today, Bishop runs on straight roads. Meditates. Eats healthy food and reads good books, makes serious studies of nature, takes hard tramps day and night through the woods. Ironically, he says the only people he's ever had any run-ins with were some old hippies who came here for a Rainbow Gathering a few years back; two or three with sticky fingers stole some of his hand tools. He says he'd like to distance himself from the pot-growing part of his past. But like Lester Simpson said, the reputation you gain in these hollers sticks like pine sap. And like it or not, when locals say that without moonshine and marijuana there'd be no Christmas in these hollers—and around here they say that an awful lot—one of the men they're thinking of, one whom they're quietly grateful for, is John Bishop. (As it turns out, Christmas may be a little lean this year after all. Old Sally Wallace has Alzheimer's, and two days ago she just up and wandered off. Searchers have been combing the woods looking for her, uncovering a lot of pot gardens along the way.)

There's water boiling on the stove, and I follow John in for a cup of tea. His carefulness, his creativity, are nowhere more obvious than in this house, a modest one-story structure covered in red oak, hand-bleached to the color of beech bark, with curves and tucks that perfectly mimic the surrounding hilltop and ravines. Large trees nestle against the decks like they're a part of the structure, as if the house was dropped from the air into a matching clearing. The floors are unstained white pine, warm and bright, and at the center of the house there's an octagon-shaped space with big pillows on the floor and glass all around, a room soaked with light and full of trees, like an aboretum.

When Bishop first came here, he worked every day, sixteen hours a day. "I loved it. It was like there was some pent-up drive in me, this need to work with my hands. I did everything the hard way: built the house on top of a mountain and literally dragged all the materials up, plus thousands of buckets of water. I made the place mostly out of recycled stuff, things I picked up in dumpsters or along the sides of county roads. Some of it came from an old house in Newport that was falling down—I got it for nothing. And then a fair number of poles from these woods, cut and peeled."

He tells me he was very much in love with the woman he came here with, that together they were tethered to this great dream, this siren song calling them to go live in the woods. At the time there was a smattering of other back-to-the-landers here from all over the country—kindred singles, couples, young families, most of them educated people who'd dropped out in the early laps of the rat race. A lot of time was spent helping one another cut wood, plant gardens, can food, put up buildings. There were birthday parties and potlucks and late nights making music with guitars and harmonicas and mandolins. But as the months went on, a lot of the newcomers felt the quiet turning heavy. The enormous effort required for the most basic tasks—washing clothes with buckets of water carried from creeks and springs, cooking without gas or electricity—started to seem less like a path than a prison. In two to five years, many of the relationships, including John's, bent under the stress, and finally broke. The immigrants scattered like November leaves.

Yet Bishop thrived. "You have to have a thirst for the work," he explains, taking the tea bag from his cup and placing it carefully in the sink. "You have to be a workaholic." He stares out the kitchen window into the forest for a long time, sipping at his tea, saying nothing. "It's just that I'm more at peace in these woods, whether it's by myself or with somebody I love, than anywhere else. It's the only place I can get a sense of there not being any boundaries between me and the rest of the world." There's a surety, a matter-of-factness, to his remark, but maybe a stab of hurt, too—like he's grateful for the strength of the leaning, but saddened by the cost.

"I spend a lot of time just sort of picking a direction and heading off in the woods to see what's there," he says. "Every time it's a trip of discovery. There's always something new and incredible. Birds, bobcat, deer and bear; turkeys, raccoon and foxes, mink. And with this rain, all the fungi—over two hundred species. After all this time, I'm still learning. A lot of times I'll go out walking in the woods in the dead of night. If I get lost, well, it's no big deal. I know how to get myself found."

We finish our tea, go back out to the deck, settle into the last hour of light. Earlier we talked a little about his birth family, how his mom and dad and siblings were these aspiring professional people, flush with the trappings of success. I can't help but wonder what they think of his life in the woods.

"It's sort of this blend of envy and curiosity and wonder.

And a little bit of disappointment. On one level, they understand it perfectly. But there's this dissonance between that understanding and the lives they lead in the suburbs—always so busy, always collecting a lot of stuff. I was the whiz kid who could have done anything, and I threw it all away.

"My brother raised a family, has a business outside of D.C.—really seems happy. But for years he's carried this secret wish to have a farm. Maybe because of that, he admires what I've done. There's also something about how much I travel. I mean, he makes six times as much as I do, but he can't get away for more than a week or two a year, and then it's to the same condo on the beach.

"But I suppose what sells everyone is that we get along better. They all know I'm happier now than ever before."

The majority of people I've met here—farmers to faith healers, moonshiners to guerrilla pot growers—many with the most modest incomes imaginable, have this easy, comfortable air about them, something that seems woven more out of tolerance than resignation, more a matter of patience than surrender. Some families have held onto these nooks and crannies at all costs—and there were times, especially as large tracts of the forest were destroyed, when the costs became obscene. Maybe the real reward of having stayed, having tended these links to the wild game and the sang, the saw timber and lobelia and pennyroyal, was that it made for a kind of evenness in life—the reassurance needed to shore up a willingness to endure, to keep stoking old stories and music and reunions. Even the religion of the hollers seems less about finding deliverance than about celebrating ties.

I spend my last night at the end of a rutted dirt road that twists for a mile through deep woods, finally petering out on the bank of the French Broad River. The place is totally without people, completely quiet, though on the weekends it's clearly a party spot, one of those hidden corners where rural kids come to drink beer and smash bottles into rocks, throw up in the sand among the willows. The recent rains have picked up a million armloads of dirt from the surrounding hills and dumped them into the river, overwhelming it, turning it into what looks like a channel of coffee and cream, stirred by the cottonwood snags it's plucked off the high banks. It has a heavy sound to it, rolling through this dark night, keeping me awake, a kind of white noise gone to black. I try to ignore it, then out of boredom, end up tracing its route in my mind, thinking of it pouring out of the hills to join the Tennessee, heading south into Alabama, finally north again, all the way through Kentucky to the Ohio River.

But in the end, that just leaves me thinking about going. And what I really want to do is stay.

Chapter Eight

Leaving east Tennessee and making for the North Woods, crossing several hundred miles of what is increasingly unforested, settled country, feels like crawling out of bed after making love to go shovel snow. For the first time on this journey, the leaving is a weight. Today even Knoxville seems overwhelming—a cluttered stream of FM and billboards and big trucks roaring westbound on I-40, leaving me shrinking in my seat like Pa Kettle on his first commute. The day after the night I reach my brother's place, we rent a pontoon boat, park it in a quiet cove of mammoth Dale Hollow Lake, twist the lid off a mason jar full of moonshine somebody gave me back in Del Rio, and sit there for an entire afternoon. It takes all that for me to stop looking behind me, southeast toward the French Broad and Cataloochee, toward Round Mountain and Max Patch, Lester and Henry and Hillbilly's.

My brother and I are the only ones left in our immediate family, parentless since our early thirties. Dad went at fifty-two, killed by his fall from that courthouse roof, Mom eight years later, from cancer, from grief. I think that's why there's a sense of ritual to our visits with one another, a re-anchoring of who we are, where we came from. We talk today of how surprised our parents might be at the way that little patch of woods they bought for their two kids to run around in every weekend sank in, even if that is just what they were hoping.

"We always thought you boys needed a place to be boys," our mother used to say. And so while our friends were back in town playing pick-up basketball at the Nuner playground and riding their bikes up Mishawaka Avenue to resupply their stock of Sweet Tarts, my brother and I were in the sticks building forts in the maples and oaks, getting into fights with sycamore fruits, slipping on our prized green waterproof boots so we could go traveling up and down the creek bottoms.

After a dozen years as a traveling salesman, Jim says he's decided to give up the road, go full-time into a landscaping business he's been building for nine months. He's more excited than I've seen him in years, talking on about the Foster holly and redbuds to be had from the wholesalers in McMinnville, about little old ladies buying day lilies from his plant stand on the bypass, about how somebody's actually growing palm trees outdoors in Quebec, Tennessee. I can't remember a time when I haven't been trying to gather up those places we roamed as kids. And now my brother, in his own way, seems to be circling back too, settling on those ten years spent on that lot with no house, helping plant blue spruce and ginko and myrtle, red maple and cardinal bush.

When I finally head north again, I find myself hopscotching from woods to woods, first through the sweetgum and hickory and hornbeam of the Big South Fork, past salmon-colored groves of river birch along the Cumberland, through small towns with names like Black Oak and Pine Knot and Greenwood. Past lands that Daniel Boone found covered in walnut and poplar, oak and hickory and sycamore, some measuring an incredible ten feet across and a hundred and fifty feet tall. Everywhere I look, there are beautiful little streams, and while these days they're as untroubled as sleeping children, a hundred years ago they were straddled everywhere with splash dams, built to catch and pool the heavy rains of spring, which in turn allowed men to float the hardwood logs they'd cut and piled along the steep banks during the previous winter. And then the dams were blasted away, sending the trees careening at breakneck speeds to the next pool—on and on, through as many as twenty dams, eventually reaching a bigger stretch of water, where they were chained into giant rafts. And finally, the best part: those rafts of logs boarded by small crews of the craziest damn river cowboys in American history—"raft devils," they were called—hired to keep an eye on things by riding on the backs of the logs, which during the early miles, at least on the Upper Cumberland, meant going through a series of roiling rapids that sometimes broke the rafts apart, sending the devils diving off their splintering ships into the torrents and swimming for their lives. Down and down into deeper, more swollen waters, sometimes covering a hundred and fifty miles of river in five or six days, usually with little or no chance for sleep.

Happily, the roads I choose are leading me back to Appalachia, in and around the Daniel Boone National Forest. To places I vaguely remember passing through years ago on our way south out of Indiana. For my mother, who was a fierce champion of the clipped lawn, scrubbed kids, and lunch-meat-at-noon crowd, this was a sad, disturbing place. A world that seemed little changed from the one she heard described when she was a kid back in the 1930s, when the government told of how in this slice of Kentucky only 6 percent of the people had running water, and only half that number had bathrooms; of how the annual cash income varied from between $40 to $280 a year. Later on, maybe squirming at the thought that it could seem so little changed, in the end I think she took the views from these back roads—the broken-down cars in the yards and the worn-out couches on leaning porches—and used them to strike a reassuring conclusion: that the only real problem here was a lack of gumption.

Then again, at the time I wasn't listening too close. All I knew was that these people had one striking advantage over the rest of us: Within arm's reach of nearly every front door we passed, there were woods and great reaches of twisted hills, cliffs and caves and fast-stepping rivers beyond the counting. I was hopelessly kidlike in thinking that the wonders of this landscape must somehow get people through, though in fact the woods did at least make an impossible life possible, if only barely. There were hardwoods to build with and sell. There was game to hunt, fruit and medicinals to gather, fish to take from the rivers.

Eventually, the idea of saving the people of Appalachia rooted in my own generation. And who could argue against the need for health-care programs in a land where 50 percent of the women suffered from some kind of chronic illness, or for better schooling in a place with 50-percent illiteracy? Yet I'm not sure we weren't driven by the same old underlying assumptions—that the poor of Appalachia needed help not so they could become more comfortable as hill folk, but so they could become more like us. Forget the rusting car parts and leaning porches. It was hard, especially for those of us busy embracing the inherent good of the open road, to even imagine the fierce desire in many Appalachian people to keep their feet planted heel-to-heel with family, preferably on the same ground where they were born. I couldn't fathom a culture where it was the exception to "get shoes" and wander from home, and even if you did, to almost always feel the need to come back.

For a generation willing to pack up and move across the country for nothing more than a shot at a good job, it was incredible to conceive of an attitude then common in the hills—that to take work elsewhere, no matter what the pay, was a kind of personal failure. We missed the fact that coal mining (which even at its peak in Kentucky never employed more than one in ten local residents) or working at sawmills were to many people annoying "hand-to-mouth" work, robbing a person of his ability to live life on his own terms. Only a fool would trade a free life for the chance to store up goods. And besides, as one Appalachian storyteller put it: "It's a lot easier to make the things you need than to make the money to buy them."

The southern reaches of Indiana north of the Ohio River are still wrapped in forests vast and rich enough to lay easy claim to the imagination: oak and maple running thick across the shoulders of the hill country, white pine standing toe-to-toe against the chalk-colored nips and tucks of the limestone hollows, sumac and fireweed nuzzling the open twists of the country roads. In the damp places of the forest are clusters of wild petunias and bee balm, the latter with shocking red blooms, faithfully tended by hummingbirds; and in the grassy openings, buckets of pale lavender bluets. From State Route 135, I can look past crumpled barns and outbuildings and conjure up huddles of young Kickapoo men, readying to hunt, invoking the spirits of the deer around an autumn fire. Or Shawnee women, coming back to gather rose hips in the warm, dry days of the blackberry moon.

The imagination game gets even easier in places where the road climbs the ridge lines, offering soaring vistas. From those places dance fleeting notions of that time long before European contact, a time, archaeologists say, when there was a sudden, inexplicable flowering of pottery, agriculture, and religion—the so-called "Woodland Period." Priests from the Fort Ancient societies standing each morning high above the Ohio River atop great earthen temple mounds, welcoming up the sun. The clans of the Delaware, who for a thousand years preserved the stories of their culture with sign-words painted on shaved sticks, one of which describes this region as a tree-laden paradise, where all kept peace with each other.

And then later, the French trappers—*coureurs de bois,* forest vagabonds. And of course the great warriors like Tecumseh, living and dying on the breath of a dream that there would one day be an inviolable Indian nation, stretching from the chestnut-covered hills of Kentucky to the dark spruce-fir forests of southern Canada. Even the first settlers who came to this part of Indiana were astonished by the wealth of the woods. "Hell," joked an old-timer I shared a cup of coffee with in Madison, "when my people got here, a squirrel could visit every tree in the state and never touch the ground." Entire cultures, blooming and fading like orchids from the forest floor.

Today much of the change travelers see as they move north through Indiana comes down to a matter of geology. By the time you cross State Road 40 outside of Indianapolis—the old National Highway—you're in pancake land, the earth filed flat some twenty thousand years ago by the grind of a glacier, the same slip of ice that turned this into such incredibly productive farmland. A gift from God, the farmers will tell you. Lots of logging and a few well-placed drainage tiles, and presto, central Indiana was on its way to becoming the golden buckle of the Midwest corn belt. It's handsome country, especially in a time when the state's open spaces are being eaten up like watermelon at the Marion Country Fair.

Yet at the same time, there's something disquieting, disappointing, in the precision of the lines, the fruit of a movement that began in the 1970s, when farmers were told in no uncertain terms to get big or get out. The lack of windmills and woodlots, cattail marshes, hedgerows and a dozen other hiccups on the horizon leaves an impression of extreme orderliness. Control. When in fact for all the chemicals and genetics, this farming thing is yet a tenuous give-and-take, a brave dance on a wet floor.

Fifty miles south of the Michigan border, at the Tri-County Wildlife Management Area, I catch my first sight of home. A loose, unconnected hodgepodge of tangled tracts with ponds and marshes and woods, among the very last things natural to be saved near the resort development of Lake Wawasee. The people living nearby don't seem to give the place much notice—except for the teenagers, of course, who have a fondness for parking at the fishing access points and drinking beer, for driving down the dirt roads and taking potshots at signs. When I was eleven, this was the edge of the known world—a place my brother and I would routinely explore by walking some eight miles one way from that piece of woods our parents bought for the family, spending the afternoon mapping it all in our heads, walking back in time for dinner.

A heron arrives at the same time I do, gliding out of a sky half the shade of her charcoal feathers to settle on the pond off Koher Road, landing behind a screen of cattails before I can scramble out of the van for a better look. There's the old familiar mix of sparrow song and the buzz of red-winged blackbirds, the sharp scent of willow and the muck of the marsh. The bluebird boxes and wood-duck platforms are still up. I walk over to a squat, disheveled tree and pluck a wild apple, bite into it, think it tastes a lot like the last one I tried somewhere near here twenty-five years ago.

Somehow, I thought it would all be gone. Turned into landfills or traded off by the counties for some right-of-way or other trinket, leveled and sold into slavery as a shopping mall. It's the way I've come to expect things will go. Probably since Mrs. Hammaker unveiled to my third-grade class the great seal of Indiana: a drawing of a settler felling trees, and in the background, the butt end of a startled bison making a mad dash to get the hell out of the way.

I don't know if the refuge permits it, but I've already decided I need to sleep here tonight—not so much for the pleasure of the night itself, but for the waking up. I'm hauling out a lawn chair, setting up to eat a little dinner, when a guy from Elkhart named Rick walks out of the woods with his rod and reel in hand, just out from bass-fishing some hidden pond a half-mile away that few people know about. We strike up a conversation and I pull out the other lawn chair for him. He's in his early thirties, tells me he's been coming to this place for ten years, that this little pond has some of the best bass-fishing anywhere, that I probably shouldn't write about it by name.

Three months ago, Rick gave up a decent factory job in Elkhart at $9.50 an hour to work as a seasonal trail boss at Chain of Lakes State Park, for $5.50. He hopes to one day parlay it into a full-time job with state or county parks, though that may take a long time. He tells me all his friends think he's out of his mind, but then I could have guessed as much. I left the state thinking Hoosiers were genetically predisposed to taking the best job as defined by the highest pay, and that they don't cotton to those who stick their noses up at the status quo. It's the old fairy-tale motif incarnate: the villagers warning about how you should never, ever leave the trodden path for the dark of the forest. I mean, it's one thing to try some harebrained scheme like Rick's when you're in your twenties—"Get it out of your system," is how they put it. But here's a guy with a wife and a little girl. A guy with responsibilities. And besides, there's always the small, but enormously irritating possibility that he'll go out and do this and actually end up happy.

I offer him a drink of my prized moonshine, kind of a celebration of his striking out on his own. It's dark and the air gets wet and the woods fill up with lightning bugs, and still we're talking about this new life of his. "I used to hate to wake up in the morning. And now I can't wait to get out of bed and start the day. How much an hour is that worth?" He tells me about the work. Says the people who come to the park love the idea of camping, but at the same time, most of them are a little afraid of it. "I think that's why people around here camp with ball games on, or the mini-TV, or some rock-and-roll station that drives their neighbors nuts. The noise is familiar—it takes the edge off all that quiet." Apparently the uneasiness grows after dark, because the campers won't walk anywhere without their flashlights. One day at dusk last week a worried-looking woman came up to Rick, wanted to know whether the rangers penned all the wild animals at night. "But at least people are coming," he says.

I have one more stop to make, this one in the heart of South Bend, my old hometown. I knock on the front door of a small white house nearly unchanged in forty years, hear some rustling-about going on inside through the open panes of glass on the porch windows, finally see the inside door open and a beautiful old woman, ninety-three, standing there on her cane, smiling, welcoming me in with a sweep of her big brown arm.

"I'm washing my walls," she tells me, maybe in response to the doubtful look she sees on my face at spotting a ladder standing in the arch between her tiny living room and kitchen. I insist on helping her but she'll hear none of it, tells me that if she doesn't keep active, she'll never be able to get going again. I shake my head, we take a seat out on the porch, where we can look down on the old street where I grew up. She tells me that tomorrow she's driving up to Michigan to help her niece can some fifty quarts of tomatoes. Pearl was next-door neighbor to my family for thirty-five years. Maybe because she and her husband didn't have children of their own, she took my brother and me on with a love that I suspect even blood relations rarely see—unconditional, a bottomless well. Sitting here, I'm thinking of how she'd have me over to help make cookies and how the flour and sugar would fly all over the place, just like the grease did when she fixed her famous fried potatoes in a big black-iron skillet, as if food was somehow less of a celebration if there wasn't some kind of mess left in its wake. For that alone I loved her. "You and Jim was always good boys," she told us, tells me again today, and she believes it so completely, says it with so much heart, that even though I know better, I can't help but think it might be true.

Pearl grew up just to the north, in Buchanan, Michigan, in hard, hard times, so in love with the outdoors that by the time she was nine she was repeatedly running away from home with her cane pole, making for her favorite lake so she could forget the world and just fish. No matter the punishment, it was never enough to keep her away for long. Besides regular hunting trips, while in her forties she and Merle bought a tiny cottage on Lake Wawasee, and from then on every summer morning they'd climb into their respective boats and motor off to spend several hours fishing. For a few years my brother and I would go stay with them for a week, Jim going out every day at 5:30 A.M. with Merle, and me with Pearl, and though I didn't even like to fish all that much I loved to fish with her.

Maybe it was payment from God for her good heart, or some kind of compensation for the hard life she'd lived on the farm, but Pearl had the astonishing privilege of reeling in fish with a kind of success virtually unknown outside biblical miracle tales. She was a big woman even then, and the sight of her in her torn, worm-smudged cotton dress jumping up in that tiny boat to wrestle some big bass or bluegill or perch from one or more of the three poles she kept going at all times, a frenzy of baiting and casting and landing—well, for a ten-year-old it was like sitting at the feet of a shaman, watching him gyrate for rain, and always getting it. To this day it remains among the most amazing, illogical things I've ever witnessed. Sometimes people in other boats would edge as close to us as they thought proper, sit there for an hour or two and get absolutely nothing, then motor away in a huff. One time a little boy about ten was in a boat nearby, having no luck himself, but at the same time having to suffer watching one of Pearl's incredible harvests going on less than two hundred feet away. Finally he looked up to see one of her fish breaking the line before she could land it. "Good!" he yelled, which made Pearl laugh until she couldn't sit up straight.

"Them was the happiest times of my life," she says.

I tell Pearl about my journey, about the birch-bark wigwam and wild man Joe Knowles, about the big trees and the moose, and even about the moonshine. I tell her that from here I'll be going north to places that she used to go on hunting trips, that I'll be following some of the same roads she took, roads my parents followed too on those precious vacations to the North Woods. Most of all, I tell her I wish she could climb in the van and go with me. So she could show me the fields where she picked strawberries at fifty cents a day, or point out the woods behind her brother's place where she used to mushroom. That maybe we could find that lake she kept running away to as a kid, or another one not far away, where she says she used to sit on a log at the shore with her sister-in-law, just to listen to the singing of the birds.

Before I leave, she heads into the basement, comes up fifteen minutes later with a box full of homemade relish, grape jam, canned beets and butter beans, a package of pork chops from her niece Margaret, four boxes of vanilla-pudding mix, and a half-bag of strawberry Newtons. Provisioning me for the trip north. "Now listen," she says over my objections, sounding stern, "I've got more than I can ever eat down there. You just take this. You'll need it."

Pearl was never religious in the traditional sense, preferring to do her visiting with the Creator while babysitting bobbers in the middle of Lake Wawasee. But she always lived by the notion that a person gets a lot more pleasure from what they give than from what they receive. I'm a hundred miles north of South Bend and still I'm looking back at Pearl's box of food sitting on the floor, wishing that I could just pull over in some patch of woods and cook up this big meal for her like she used to do for me, that I could turn the burner on the camp stove up real high and toss in the pork chops and just let the grease fly.

One minute the road is lined with cornstalks rising out of black dirt, the next with bracken, wintergreen, sarsaparilla, and plantations of red pine, the latter planted much like the corn was, feet standing in soil sandy as a cat box. How is it that the same miles that seemed to take such a big bite out of life when I was a kid making for the North Woods could today be flying by so fast? As eager as I am to make it across the Mackinac Bridge and roll onto Michigan's Upper Peninsula, into the land of Kirkland's warblers and the Two-Hearted River, I force myself to slow down well short of all that, pull in for a stroll around Loda Lake. It's a small, precious wildlife sanctuary in the Huron-Manistee National Forest, a high-school biology teacher's dream, and one of the last places left for miles around with anything close to the mix of plants that would have grown here a hundred and fifty years ago—in part, no doubt, because in that same period, over half of Michigan's wetlands have been filled or drained. Remarkably, there's not a soul around, just me and the beaver and muskrat, all of us wrapped in a weave of plants I haven't had a good honest visit with for fifteen years. There's jack-in-the-pulpit and swamp rose, spring beauty and trillium, sarsaparilla and squirrel corn, cinnamon fern and dewberry and fragrant water lilies. White violets and Carolina rose.

Hiding in the shade are the thick, shiny leaves of periwinkle, though their perfect lavender flowers are at least a month gone. Like a lot of exotics, periwinkle was carried here from Europe—not by accident but on purpose, by the sackful even, toted across the Atlantic by immigrants who cherished it as a medicinal to stop bleeding, to regulate blood pressure, and as a better-than-average treatment for nervous disorders. Acknowledging one of its Old World names, Violet of the Sorcerers, many of those same newcomers also hung it above their doors to ward off bad magic, just as they hid pennies under windowsills to bring good luck.

Here too in fair abundance is a native plant wearing purplish blooms, each in the shape of a visored military helmet known to the New England colonists as a "skullcap"—the name the flower still bears today. It was skullcap they found Indian tribes using as a sedative, a practice they took to in short order. Herbalists continue to prescribe it not only for that—some, because it contains an antispasmodic, suggest it as a means of controlling epileptic seizures.

Being that I'm here during midday, there are fresh drops of sap beaded on the hairs of dish-shaped leaves at the base of the sundew plants. I lie on the ground beside one and wait, and sure enough, in a matter of minutes an unsuspecting insect comes along, can't resist what looks like the sparkle of something good to eat, crawls in for a taste. The hairs curl over it, more sap is released—really a digestive protein—and it's the plant that ends up getting the meal. A good strategy for getting by, especially when you live in nutrient-poor soils. Sundew too has been a highly valued medicinal for at least seven hundred years; it was used widely throughout England to treat the violent coughing jags that come with tuberculosis, and is still used today to soothe whooping cough.

At some invisible line south of Baldwin, trees suddenly grip the road, and tourist and sportsmen's shops explode out across the landscape. Signs advertise trout-fishing ponds and canoe trips and cabins, and rooms to rent at places like "The

Wonderland Motel" and the "Pine Tree Lodge," with laminated color-photo placemats on the desks and real drinking glasses wrapped in stiff white paper sitting on the back of porcelain sinks; churches that offer campfire services every weekend of the summer; hunting clubs; bars with huge, gaping-mouthed fish hanging from the walls; bait shops with buckets of minnows for those after muskie and pike. Even the convenience stores have outdoorsy names: the "Whitetail Quick Mart," the "Lakeland Stop and Go."

And then that glorious bridge across the straits of the Mackinac, hoisting you up over a great blue sweep of water and then setting you down in the Upper Peninsula. Once across, you see that the forests along the road grow older, forty or fifty years from the saw, more wild and ragged-looking, more frequently dotted with bogs and blueberries and twisted, tea-colored rivers, thick with the smell of pine and tamarack and peat. There's no mistaking the fact that from this point on, westward all the way across northern Wisconsin and Minnesota, this was and is logging country. Maine was king of the timber heap until about 1850, after which the industry pulled up stakes and moved the bulk of its operations to New York, where it stayed through the 1850s; then on to Pennsylvania through the 1860s, and finally to Michigan, Wisconsin, and Minnesota, which ruled the roost from 1870 until about 1900. (Both southern Appalachia and the Pacific Northwest remained small players until well after 1900.)

In 1847, Dan Stanchfield, a timber cruiser working along the Rum River, climbed the highest tree and felt his jaw drop. The pine along fifty miles of the main watercourse, he said, reached from the shore on each side as far as the eye could see. "I had seen pine that seventy mills could not cut in as many years, although I had seen but a small part of it." Even today, as likely as not you'll take breakfast at a diner called "The Lumberjack," buy your hardware at Timber John's, and fill up the tank at Stump Junction; drink a couple of rounds on Friday night, eat a pasty, dance on a pinewood floor at the Deadfall Lounge.

Though the big trees are long gone, it doesn't take much to imagine these dark conifer woods filled with them again. For that matter, filled with ten to fifteen thousand lumberjacks, strong and burly, working in hundreds of camps scattered throughout these northern woods. Some of them had come willingly, others had fallen for the smooth talk and bright promises of a "man stealer," a guy with a wad of timber company cash who went to cities like Milwaukee and Duluth, plied young men with drinks, loaded them on trains and took them off to the winter woods.

It never was a job for the fainthearted. You slept in an open room two to a bunk, wrapped in a pair of wool blankets they gave you the day you signed in. Mornings began with two distinct jolts, the first being the sound of the bull cook screaming out, "Daylight in the swamp, boys!" and the next when you trudged out through forty-below weather to the cook shack to stuff yourself with breakfast. And while it's true that morning and night you could eat all you wanted, the bad news was that you were given only fifteen minutes to do it in. Nor could you warm yourself with a little friendly conversation, since talking meant that the guy holding his plate over his head yelling for more "sweat pads" (pancakes, in lumberjack lingo) might not get heard by the cookie stationed up front who was supposed to be shoveling out seconds and thirds on the food. Get caught talking and the head cook might throw you out, and he could do it, because the cook was king.

After breakfast, it was off to the woods through the cold, murky light of dawn, four to a team: an undercutter to notch the tree to show what direction to fell it, a pair of sawyers to cut it down, a swamper to take off the limbs and mark the trunk every sixteen feet, the sawyers then back again to cut it into lengths. The logs were placed on sleighs in loads that weighed twenty-five tons, pulled out over frozen road ruts by a single pair of horses. Even the roads in logging country—some seven or more miles of them in a typical five-hundred-acre camp—were a kind of work of art, carefully re-iced during the night with barrels of water from the river to keep them smooth and flat and fast.

So it went six days a week. On Sunday, you could sleep in a little, even take a bath of sorts if you chose to, though not many did, using a tub of hot water from what the bull cook was boiling up to wash the linens. Some Sundays you might even get a visit from that famous sky-pilot preacher Frank Higgins, who slid into camps all over this country on his tiny sleigh pulled by two Saint Bernards. Stood there straight and tall on a stump in his plaid wool shirt and logging pants, set about saving the souls of some of the roughest characters America has ever known.

Chapter Nine

What I never expected, what leaves me stumbling for balance, are the echoes from the past held in the smell of the Minnesota forest. This perfect blend of balsam and spruce and jack pine and aspen, picking the locks on some long-forgotten door to memory, flooding me with thoughts of being in the North Woods twenty-five years ago. Fourteen, at that piney rental cabin with the steel-spring chairs on the porch where you can sit and look over the tops of the conifers to the piers on Sand Lake. Early morning with my dad and brother in a small green fishing boat, the Johnson motor singing through its nose, trailing thin lines of blue smoke. Fish and potatoes frying in a skillet half the size of the electric range, eating from unmatched plates on a red Formica table. Out on the porch after dinner, after dark, a yellow lightbulb burning against streams of lightning bugs—my mother's pale legs poking out of her navy-blue shorts, her hand over her mouth, laughing.

Long after nothing persists and the people are dead,

Proust said, after things are broken and scattered, the smells and the tastes stay poised, every drop holding the vast structure of recollection. It feels like my head is about to explode. What amazes me even more than details of the events are the jolts of old appetites: pestering my parents to stop so we can walk down some twisted, overgrown fire road through the jack pine; hurrying out of the car at every gas station to collect more road maps, and then sitting in the backseat with them, figuring out how long it would take—and exactly how much money—to ride my bicycle the four hundred miles from home back to these woods. Then, back in South Bend, rushing down to the River Park Library for a copy of *The Long-Shadowed Forest* or *A Place in the Woods* or some other book by Helen Hoover, an author who in 1954 left Chicago to take up summer residence in a tiny cabin near the north shore of Lake Superior. Each volume with a splash of pen-and-ink drawings of deer and birch trees, and canoes skittering across some rockbound lake.

More and more I'm beginning to think the first half of life is like a beautiful piece of pottery that seems destined to either shatter under tragedy or crumble under the weight of worry and fear. Maybe the second half is about scouring the landscape for those lost pieces, those chips of spirit, combing them out of the grass with your fingers, figuring out a way to piece them together, make something beautiful again.

Well north of Duluth, in a toss of conifers and old Finnish homesteads, I turn onto a half-mile-long two-track, coast through a tunnel of white spruce, aspen, balsam and birch, come to rest at a place called "Winter Moon." There's a long line of dog pens at the edge of the yard bursting with huskies, twenty-eight in all. A few offer halfhearted barks, but for the most part they pay little attention to me, preferring to lie low, splayed out like piles of laundry, panting through the ninety-degree heat. From the far end of a small yard cradling an old Finnish log cabin, a woman with auburn hair is approaching, smiling and calling out a hello, calming the one or two anxious dogs with a voice like that of a mother to her children. She's Kathleen Anderson—dog-sled musher, carpenter, outfitter for a variety of all-women adventures from sled-dog treks to sea kayaking. She offers a firm, callused hand, and the smile on her tan, slightly freckled face is relaxed, as if she just this minute got up from a long nap. I'd guess she's around forty, but in truth she's one of those outdoor women whose age may have somehow been blurred by having been so long in nature, whose walk and wave of hand hold a kind of youthful grace, an effortlessness, as if her body had picked up the movements of the things around her—quiet water, rustling leaves, deep snow.

The friend in Duluth who told me about Kathleen said that of all the people he knows, she's the one with the most unabashed love for the North Woods. So I called her up, told her I was trying to meet people tied to the woods, as many as I could, people who know things the rest of us have forgotten about living with the land. We make our way to a patch of shade in the middle of the yard, she hands me two ceramic coffee mugs, goes a few rounds on an old hand pump while I hold the cups under the spout. She says she's been thinking about what I said on the phone and that she's still not sure what I'm looking for. I say I'm not sure either, but that at this point I've been on the road long enough to hope to recognize it when it comes along. Or that maybe now it's just a matter of believing I'll find something special, and so I do. She smiles, nods her head.

We finish off our second mug of well water, she asks if I'd like a tour. We begin just off the yard on the far side of a loose patch of woods, at a sauna house she just finished building, then move on to the bunkhouse where her guests stay—a solid, comfy-looking bungalow filled with single beds, built years ago with her ex-husband Jim. In the yard itself there's a fine rock garden, and beside it a jack pine she planted for shade seventeen years ago, all grown up now into something almost stately. And then the house. A beautiful little saltbox cabin of tamarack and spruce, the logs hand-cut with dovetailed corners, Finnish style, the outer walls turned gray as granite by some seventy winters, softened around the foundation by lines of flowers. The inside is plain, restful; in the kitchen there's a pine table, and open shelves filled with canned goods. A bed with an end table. Books. Candles. A boom box.

"It was trashed when we came here. Every window broken out, nothing but a hunting shack, really. We jacked the whole house up and replaced the bottom logs, put in a new foundation, floor joists, sandblasted all the interior walls, sanded the beams. Put in a new floor. A new roof."

I notice there are no power lines.

"I just got solar!" she says, eyebrows raised, flashing a big grin. "For lights and electric. I put in this thousand-watt inverter. In winter, I sometimes have to charge the batteries once in a while with my little generator, the sun is so low, but in summer, there's plenty to spare. I lived here sixteen years without any power. I have to say I like it." She points out a small television and VCR, used mostly for showing how-to sled-dog videos to the women on her mushing trips, and maybe for an occasional nature program. "And 'Northern Exposure,' " she adds. "I always thought that was one of the better shows."

When Kathleen Anderson got out of college some eighteen years ago, she kicked off her life not by heading for the woods, but for Chicago, working in a VISTA rehab center for the chronically mentally ill. Later, accompanied by a good friend whom she would eventually marry, she made her way north back to her home state, to Minneapolis, where she and Jim set up house in a group home for delinquent teenagers. "Basically, I was twenty-two years old and I had ten kids. And that was when we bought this place. We thought it would make a perfect getaway for the boys." Several years later, when she and Jim began to feel burned out at the group home, they turned in their notices, though a little reluctantly, and came up here to this old cabin in the woods for a vacation. For a time-out. That was seventeen years ago. Jim is long gone to Duluth, squeezed out by the isolation of the place, drawn by the need for a career. Two other partners have come and gone as well.

But by all appearances, Kathleen is thriving. She reminds me of women I knew out in Idaho who were working the fire towers, women who'd come down those steel staircases for the last time in the fall and shake their heads, say in a sad voice how the time always went so fast for them, talk about the books they didn't get to read, all the letters they meant to write but never found the time for.

"This was never a fad for me," Kathleen says. "You stay in the woods for the long haul only if it's something you value deeply. You have to want it. There've been a lot people move in since I've been here, and all but a small core group are gone. There's the daily chores, the trudging to the outhouse. Every time you want to wash the dishes, clean up, you pump water and then heat it with wood you've cut. Things break down and you don't always have the money to fix them, and even if you do, it's thirty miles to town for parts. But this has always been my first priority. To live here. To not need a lot of things."

It occurs to me that maybe what made so many of the people who came here twenty years ago pack up and leave wasn't the amount of work per se, but the way you have to pour yourself into the smallest inconveniences, giving no thought as to whether or not they stretch into all-day affairs. Kathleen says it's really just a matter of perspective, of what drives your life. "It's one thing if your car breaks down and you're on the freeway and you have to get to work. But it's something else entirely if it breaks down on a peaceful country roadside and a neighbor comes along and says, 'Can I help? Do you need a lift home? Do you need a job?' " That's the payoff, she says. Time enough to find your place in the community. Space enough for making small adjustments, year by year, on your own behalf. Enough quiet so as to not be easily distracted.

The guests range in age from fourteen to almost seventy. From all over the country, some returning year after year, telling one friend and then another. Women who are not in any sense adrift or wondering what to do with their lives, but dynamic people, mostly professionals, who feel the need to get back to present time, who know the value of breaking routine, of once in a while taking a big hammer and shattering the predictability of their lives. Feed and water and harness the dogs, drive the sled, build the fires. Get up in the middle of the night at twenty below, make tea and call the neighbors, help one another up onto the roof to watch the northern lights flashing in the winter sky.

I've decided to tramp these woods by water, alone in a canoe through the Boundary Waters, maybe find a patch or two of big pines that somehow escaped the lumberman's saw. It's been raining like some kind of punishment. Shortly after dawn this morning a massive thunderstorm roared through, toppling trees all over Ely, killing two canoeists, gunning them down with a single bolt of lightning while they were struggling to keep their camp from blowing away. As for me, I'm waiting it out twenty-some miles up the Echo Trail, parked next to a pot of coffee in the home of sled-dog outfitters Charlie and Connie Cowden. They've been showing off their latest home improvement—a massive wooden tower beside the house, a huge cistern on top, fed by the rain gutters, holding water that's then forced down by gravity into the kitchen faucets.

"Our first running water," Connie says proudly. "Just for washing, though, and of course not in the winter." In winter, water still comes from mile-long round-trips by dog sled to the spring. With no electricity propane works fine to cook with and to run the newly acquired refrigerator, and oil lamps provide reasonable light. It's a beautiful home, a two-story, hand-built medley of pine, the walls hung with moose and deer antlers and marten and beaver pelts. The kitchen is spacious and full of green light, and the shelves are heavy with bags of wild rice harvested last summer, and rows and rows of canning jars filled with everything from beaver to blueberries. As much as anyone I've met, Charlie and Connie draw their livelihood from the woods: food from wild game and various other kinds of native harvests; cash from running trap lines and outfitting sled-dog trips, mostly for people from Minneapolis and Chicago.

Surprisingly, what to me seems like an amazing degree of self-sufficiency, Charlie, at least today, makes out to be a tepid compromise. At thirty-five he's devoted most of his life to realizing a childhood obsession for living off the land, and now the battle seems half lost, a casualty of civilization creeping farther and farther into the woods. It's outrageous to him that the government should dictate when he can take a moose to feed his family and when he can't. Who would know more about the population of moose or any other native animal, he asks indignantly—when it's okay to hunt or trap certain species and when to back off, whether to take a moose calf this year or a cow—than someone who spends all his time in the woods? (Charlie also has a degree in Wildlife Science, though he never mentions it.)

"Let me give you an example," he says. "Over the years I've found the number of beaver I can trap and still keep the population level, healthy—about a hundred over a hundred and fifty square miles, and only two from a single lodge. Some lodges I've trapped for eight years at those numbers and the populations have stayed exactly the same. Don't forget, somebody who knows what they're doing can look at the size of a lodge, the size of the food cache, and tell you about how many animals there are. I've always managed for the long term. The guys you have to worry about are the ones who get into it only when the prices are high, just stop off the roads and wipe out an entire lodge.

"The wilderness thing, it would've been possible even thirty or forty years ago," he says. "In the early sixties there were still some people who just took up their packs, some rudimentary tools, and walked off into the wilderness and built a cabin on some unnamed lake. To me, that was the ideal—to be free in a land that was plentiful. But the white man is so damn greedy. And now we have all these regulations. I hate the rules, they drive me nuts. But I also know that without them all of this would be gone—the woods clear-cut, the game hunted out. In this society there's no balance. We grab at everything. Here you either win big or end up a loser."

I meet a lot of people who say they were born too late. Charlie really was.

The three of us huddle around the kitchen table and peruse a couple of family photo albums. There are pictures of curtains of pelts hanging from the porch at the end of trapping season, right before bundling and shipping them off to market; of little kids smiling under balsam trees; of sled-dog trips to Loon Lake, where Charlie and Connie are helping a burly looking man named Freddy cut out two hundred blocks of ice from the lake and pack them away for the summer tourist trade. "The only place that goes through twenty thousand pounds of ice for whiskey," Freddy likes to say. Pictures of old guys and old women with faces chiseled by a long string of long winters. Some are gone, and that makes the photos more precious still.

As we peruse the albums I keep making comparisons between Charlie Cowden and Kathleen Anderson, the founder of Winter Moon. Though each has a strong love of mushing, as well as an uncanny knack for finding comfort in long days spent at grueling physical labor, at first glance it might seem they couldn't be more different—she with her quiet rituals of celebration, out in a sea kayak with a handful of women singing up the full moon, he in a wall tent with a bunch of guys from Chicago, frying up beaver, telling dirty jokes. But the striking thing they have in common is this drive to keep rooting themselves deeper into the land by weaving relationships with neighbors—especially old neighbors, many of whom see the world far differently than they do.

I used to hear people in the outback talk about their fondness for their neighbors and think yeah, right. I mean, what choice do you really have? The guy next door could be an ax murderer and if you end up deathly sick, it's still his door you're going to find yourself knocking on. The mere thought of it can seem suffocating to those who learned that you meet kindred souls by moving around, joining the right clubs, getting your kids into this school or that one. There are of course people out here who qualify as honest-to-goodness hermits. But in general, the more you appreciate the land, the more you're likely to get to know the old folks around you, because knowing them lets you more fully understand the environment. It's a sense of place sprouted from a slow, patient understanding of the tracks that nature made in people's lives, and both Charlie and Kathleen have it. Kind of like learning to sail so you can better understand the wind. Each has spent countless long hours around this woodstove or that one listening to stories, refusing to separate humans from the woods, sensing the folly of trying to ever become truly rooted if you embrace nothing but snow and stars and wolves howling in the night. Around here, memories get traded like recipes across the cold winter nights. And in time, that turns strangers into something that looks a lot like family.

The sky finally brightens a bit, and it's long past time for me to go. "Keep your food up," Charlie says when we reach the entry point and start unloading my equipment. "Plenty of black bears." And then he offers a bizarre story to prove it. "Quite a few years ago, it was. Couple of instructors just dropped off this Outward Bound student for his solo, were paddling away when they heard him screaming like hell. Turned back and saw this black bear had him by the neck—was trying to drag him into the lake and drown him—so they raced over, jumped ashore and beat it off with paddles. A week later this bear does the same thing to some other guy—tries to drown him like before. Anyway, they hunted it down and it was just skin and bones. Opened it up and found the gut lined with plastic—camp trash. Poor guy couldn't digest anything. He was starving to death."

The outbound river takes its sweet time, swaying back and forth like someone dancing to old jazz records, all neck and hips. The edges are framed by arrowhead pickerelweed, and long runs of pink-and-white bullhead and tuberous lilies, the latter with blooms opening and closing at each rise and fall of the sun.

Between the put-in and the Pauness lakes is an amazing cross section of people: young families with sunburned thighs, dads with potbellies grunting under their rental canoes; boys in their late teens carrying enormous backpacks and even full-sized coolers, looking strong and heroic for their girlfriends, a number of whom, remarkably, are still wearing makeup and earrings. And of course Scout Troops, which, depending on the leader, can look like short marines or a gaggle of misfits. But after several portages the population shifts. Except for the ubiquitous Scout Troops, the groups get smaller, calmer. A father and son, the occasional couple in their thirties wrapped in Gore-tex, one or two lone paddlers.

My last conversation of the day comes mid-afternoon, with a big, friendly guy around fifty in canvas pants and an army T-shirt—a blue-collar fisherman, you could say, lived in Ely all his life. He very much approves of the fact that I'm not really sure of my plans (unlike a couple of troop leaders I met, who seemed to think me either lazy or foolhardy, treating my lack of planning as a kind of offhanded slap against the Scout motto). "Take your time," this lone paddler advises. "Get in too much of a hurry and you'll turn it into work. And there's already too much of that." He goes on to tell me of how America is becoming nothing but a giant labor camp—people working eighty hours a week. "And for what?," he asks, pausing to cock his head, like I might really have an answer. "I'm telling you, no other country lives like that." He proceeds to give me the skinny on a few choice fishing holes—the surest way to slow down is to sit around waiting for the fish, he assures me—then tosses a worn, dry bag into the bow of his canoe and readies to push off for home.

"I tried to move to Montana last year," he says in parting. "Just part-time, you know—someplace with milder winters. Too expensive, though. Guess the mountains are out of reach for guys like me." He looks back once from offshore, tilts his head up at me, a friendly gesture. Likely he's mistaken my standing around shuffling from one foot to another, thinking up excuses to put off this portage, as being properly deliberate.

At Loon Lake, four men in two boats have stolen across the invisible line across which motors are forbidden, are anchored there, fishing in the calm of a bay. One of them spots me a good half-mile off, and immediately the lines and the anchors come in, the engines sputter to life and they head west. Like I was some kind of canoe cop. From what people tell me there's no love lost between paddlers and power boaters. When I asked Charlie Cowden about stopping over to see his friend Freddy who cuts ice out of Loon Lake, he thought it was a great idea. But he changed his mind fast when he remembered I'd be traveling by canoe. "Better not, or you'll get a raft of shit," he warned, sure of it, like he'd seen it before. "I can just hear old Freddy: 'Well, la-di-da. And who are you? Wait—don't tell me—you're following the path of the goddamned voyagers!" Still, it's tempting, if only for a chance at a tumblerful of Scotch over chips of lake ice. But in the end I carry on northward, reaching the top of East Loon Lake a couple of hours before dusk.

The camp rests in a modest grove of white spruce and jack pine, dwarfed here and there by the towering pouf of an old white pine that somehow escaped the saw. Every time I see these old giants I can't help but imagine what this land must have looked like a hundred and fifty years ago: red and white pines so big you couldn't see the tops, their trunks pruned of branches for fifty or sixty feet. A floor clean and spacious enough to drive a wagon through, except where some old giant had toppled over in a windstorm, kicking off a race of saplings. And always this great hush, birdsong and deer hooves and even the clumsy ways of men soaked up by a six-inch carpet of needles. In most of the north today when conifers are cut they're not even replanted, let alone allowed to reach middle-age. Today's markets are pushed by paper waferboard, which means letting pioneer trees like aspen and birch run up dense patches of suckers—the first stage of forest succession—then mowing them down and tossing them into the chipper. On and on, until you drain the nutrient base, which is no big deal because there're always fertilizers. Logging for the lazy.

I'm planted lakeside atop a slab of granite, making notes and dreaming of dinner, when I hear a rustling behind me, moving through the deep woods out toward the shore. I'm about to rise, hoping to creep to the fringe of the forest for a better look, when some forty feet away a coyote pokes its head through a curtain of pin cherry. We stare at one another for five or ten seconds, then it slowly turns and walks back into the woods. A few minutes later I hear it farther down the shore, letting out a couple of yips and yodels, immediately followed by the cry of a loon. After this come long bursts of both creatures singing at the same time—unreal. Charging the mix even more is the fact that every last note is repeated a second or so later, nearly as clear and crisp as the original, running back to me as echoes off a line of granite cliffs on the far side of the lake. When the coyote finally quits, the loon tosses out a few more bars and then it grows silent, too. It's all I can do not to stand up on my rock and applaud.

I wake up the next day to rain smooching with the birch leaves, dripping off to drum on the slabs of rock and the fly of the tent. In a way I'm tired of all this wet, but on the other hand I'm thankful for the excuse to roll over and go back to sleep. As usual, I have no watch on, but by the time I pack up, grab a bite, and shuttle over to work the first portage, it's probably closing in on eleven. The first carry of the day goes fine, but the second one, well, there's where I end up doing something stupid. Outdoor writer Michael Furtman has told me about this wonderful old abandoned portage he took several years ago, leading into a perfect little lake that few people ever get to. "You may kill me for even suggesting this trail," he admits. "I've no idea what kind of shape it's in." Well, after some serious looking, I manage to find the portage, but then—and this is the stupid part—I end up walking the entire length of it, a mile and a quarter, all the way to the next lake without carrying a thing, drawn on by some obsessive need to convince myself that this is really the right path. So instead of walking five miles over downed logs and through the thickets in two trips, I do seven and a half miles in three.

The good news is that I'm beginning to get more comfortable with carrying the canoe, having figured out that by pushing my elbows up and against the thwart I can increase the amount of arm and shoulder available for the pads to rest on, which makes things hurt a lot less. When I get really desperate I stick my head up against the bottom of the boat, stretching my neck like a singing loon, taking the weight on my noggin. But that trick is less than worthless on uneven ground, since then the Royalex starts rippling and bouncing like a tire against my skull. No matter how long I do this canoe thing I'll always feel like a weenie, given that the old trappers east of here routinely shouldered three ninety-pound bundles at once and carried them nine miles around Grand Portage, and did it in less time than it takes me to go four miles with sixty.

Camp is set and I'm down at the shore, rinsing sweat out of my T-shirt, when some forty or fifty yards behind me a loon pops up and lets out a loud yodel. I can't say what makes me read this as an invitation, but without thinking twice I drop the shirt, slip on my life jacket and ease into the water. Ever so slowly I paddle toward her, out into the middle of the lake. Each time she calls out I answer back in what seems even to me a horrible falsetto warble, half expecting her to either flush or paddle over and peck out my vocal chords. But no, she stays right where she is, just keeps on calling. Twenty yards away I stop, at which point her mate starts chiming in from over on the far shore, then begins to move our way. She swims over and greets him, maybe whispers something about me that piques his curiosity, because pretty soon both of them return, one on each side of me. And there the three of us stay for a good fifteen minutes, they on their bellies and me on my back, the two of them singing back and forth like angels from some wild heaven and me chortling like, well, something less.

Between choruses, I lie there and watch the clouds drift across the sky, gray and sticky-looking, sunbeams drilling through the holes and then withdrawing. On the shore, millions of aspen and birch leaves are fluttering in a light breeze.

Chapter Ten

The mosquitoes have this routine they run through every evening about eight o'clock, hanging back just long enough to let me think I've finally found a place where they won't bother me, then all at once descending in one big grainy, whining cloud. At first I give in, hang out in the tent reading Sigurd Olson, laugh at them through the screen. But I quit all that at the point I find out how easily they can be left behind simply by climbing in the canoe and giving a few easy paddle strokes away from shore.

Truth is, I owe those mosquitoes, because this nighttime canoeing thing is fast becoming one of my favorite activities. (Lately I've been seriously thinking about laying out my sleeping bag on the bottom of the boat and spending the night out there, hull-to-breast with the loons.) On calm nights, in places with a good wood supply, I light a small blaze in the fire ring and then glide out into the darkness, going as far as I can and still see the winking of the flames, eventually moving back through the black, working to not make a drip or a whisper with the paddle, feeling like I'm piloting a space ship toward a distant star. One night an almost perfectly round hole broke open in the clouds and moonlight poured onto the lake, forming a beam of soft blue-white light fanning out from the bow of the canoe.

Thanks to the almost complete lack of wind, there are other, equally astonishing special effects to be had here. On several occasions in late evening, the surface of the lake has gotten flat as a mirror, reflecting not only rosy puffs of cumulous clouds, but every gull and nighthawk flying overhead. By focusing my gaze slightly ahead and to the side, it's possible to nurture the astonishing illusion that I'm looking down through clouds from someplace high above the earth. And that yields, at least for a second or two, the rather gut-spinning feeling that I'm paddling through the sky. Like if the canoe tipped over, I'd tumble down through ten thousand feet of clouds.

The farther out I go, the fewer people I see—just one party, a father and son, in the past two days. Time blurs into a blissful routine of paddle and portage, broken now and then by long swims under smoke-colored granite cliffs; head-down shuffles along the mud looking for sign of bear and deer, mink and coyote; lunches taken afloat, sitting in thick curtains of wild rice.

Though there aren't many trails outside the portage paths, there's no end of opportunity for fine, aimless rambles through the woods. In a few places I've found great stretches of the forest floor completely covered in three-inch carpets of moss, perfectly laid from tree to tree and green as Ireland. Elsewhere are pockets of slack water filled with fragrant water lilies and sheets of aquatic grasses, all of it rimmed at the edges by clusters of black spruce. It's in these places that I begin to hear the unmistakable murmur of the boreal forest, where I get this knee-buckling, breathtaking urge to paddle farther, on into Lac La Croix and past Twentyseven Island, up the Namakan to the Quetico.

North. Farther and farther north. On returning to the canoe after such discoveries the only thing to do is to spend a few minutes hovering over my Fisher maps, with their great toss of islands and twists of water leaking everywhere. Wallow a little in the possibilities.

It's not surprising that such a twisted, labyrinth-like wilderness, a place of shadowy woods and pocket gardens and stony niches beyond the counting, would be rich with myth, and over the centuries the Ojibwa made it so. From the rockbound lakes to the heart of forest, even in the way geese flow across the northern sky, can be found reminders of the exploits of their great creator-magician Nanabozho, son of the West Wind and great-grandson of the Moon. And other tales too, like when the Great Spirit helped Nanabush make the first butterflies. It was the fluttering of those beautiful winged creatures that so delighted the twin human babies born to Spirit Woman, causing them to reach and stretch and strain in an effort to catch them, which is how children first learned to walk. Again, mythical images flowed from the Ojibwa to the arrivals from the Old World, the most obvious example being Longfellow's rendition of an Ojibwa Nanabozho story, which he called "The Song of Hiawatha." Once again the newcomers seemed to find the stories they carried across the Atlantic from their native England and Europe to be strangely incomplete here, inadequate to let them sing the experience of this wild new land.

On my way west to Boundary Waters, I had the privilege of visiting for the better part of an afternoon with Amelia Legarde, an Ojibwa elder and storyteller. We sat together in the sun-filled living room of her big yellow house, nestled in Duluth on a quiet street in a long row of Victorian houses, the sound of maple leaves and the smell of Lake Superior rolling through the windows. Around us were photographs of strong-looking grandmothers and smiling grandchildren, and on the wall above the floral couch where we sat, a print of a gnarly old conifer—"a spirit tree," Amelia called it—

perched on the shore rocks of the Grand Portage Reservation. On another wall a small painting of an Eskimo sitting in a kayak, and beside that, a collage of other images from the far north cut from magazines and carefully matched in a single frame—a tribute to this mysterious draw Amelia has to the Eskimos, as if in another life she was right there with them, hunting seals on the ice. And finally, on the dining-room table, her latest project: one of the most striking beaded vests I've seen, nearly finished, jet-black cloth with flower heads in the sacred colors of white and red, round and bell-shaped, each one resting atop long green stems that seemed to sway against the fabric, like seaweed in the current. I remember thinking how well the images on the vest matched Amelia's voice—deep and rich and full of color. A storyteller's voice.

One of the things we talked about is this trade in woodland myth between settlers and the Ojibwa. And again, just like Barry Dana of the Maine Penobscots, Amelia felt that the swapping grew out of good relations with the French. "The French people seemed to recognize the American Indians as kindred spirits," she explained. "They had a certain joy for life that our people have also. We're told that our relations with the French were those of acceptance, fellowship, even love."

But while most newcomers (mainly trappers and other people of the woods) were only too happy to take clues about the wilderness from the Indians, some of the black-robed priests seemed intent on burning out all native myth in a fire of Christianity. Over time, the Indian people themselves grew sharply divided over whether to be traditional or fully Catholic, a rift that turned brother against brother, mother against son, and continues even to this day. Amelia was exposed to Catholicism as a child, both in the majority-white school she attended off the reservation and by a lone missionary who came once a month to her village.

"He took confession on Saturday," she recalled, "then

promised on Sunday that if God didn't take us, the devil would. All the most faithful gathered and felt holy for that one day. But the people who went to church who were also traditional Indians, their worship never stopped. It was—it still is—an everyday thing."

She says she's grateful to have lived among people who would not abandon the old ways. "One of the few nice memories I have of childhood is waking up at dawn to the sound of my father's voice. He's out back, out past the east-facing door of this one-room shack where the five of us lived, giving thanks in Ojibwa for another day. Then he would come inside and say, 'My children, get up! There's another new day coming!' And that's how we started our morning."

Then it was off to school—complete with history lessons, she says, about how evil her ancestors were, how they murdered and burned the good missionaries who brought them this great religion. "To tell the truth, it got into my mind. But in the background there was always the sound of my father giving thanks for another day. Eventually, through a lot of turmoil, the spirituality I learned as an Indian person, and that I held to so dearly as a child, came back. Throughout my life I had seen some people who could balance their Catholicism with their Indian philosophy without hurting themselves spiritually. These were the kinder people on the reservations. But this was not something I could do.

"I was taught that the earth is our mother—that the mountains and hills are the forms of her body, that the streams and rivers are her blood, that the forest is her hair. My father made part of his living by cutting wood, and sometimes he would take me with him into the woods. And always before he would start chopping a tree, he would put a gift at the base. He would say, 'Thank you that you're going to help me feed my children.' Always with respect. Those limbs were not left just lying around, they were stacked into neat piles. A way of being thankful to nature, centuries old, that lived on in my father. Today in some parts of the Indian world there are places where timber doesn't grow anymore. Where it's been . . . murdered, really. Three years ago, across the street from my house here, there was a beautiful old maple tree, and they said its roots were interfering with the plumbing of the houses. And so it was cut down. I watched them do it, and oh, that hurt. I waited for a quiet time and I went over and spread some tobacco. I told it that it had served the people well. I told it that it was beautiful."

In the Ojibwa world, Amelia says, all the trees were sacred. But four were especially important. "There was the maple tree, whose sap provided us with one of our staples at the beginning of food-gathering in the spring. The cedar we used in our spiritual practices. And the poplar and the birch we used in many ways. There's a story about how the birch came to be such a helper to the Ojibwa. Nanabozho was a strong spirit who came to the people to teach them how to live on this earth. At that time, the animals and the people communicated well, sometimes to the point where it was hard to tell where the human left off and the four-legged, or the winged creature, or the scaled creature, began. Though he could transform himself into whatever he wanted to, Nanabozho also had all the qualities of the human being. He could be bad or good, generous or stingy, happy or sad, he could love and hate. Well, one day he was in his mischief-making mood—as he was growing up, he found this mood to come upon him more often than his teaching side. He was out walking in the woods, enjoying the forest, when up ahead he spotted a mountain. And on this mountain was a tall pine tree, and near the top was the nest of an eagle—a thunderbird. Now this piqued his curiosity. He could see one of the eagle parents up there, and he told himself that when it was gone, he would climb up to the top. So sure enough, the parents left and he climbed up and found two baby eagles. He was about to grab one when the parents returned, frightening him, sending him half-climbing and half-falling down the tree. The eagles were very angry and kept diving at him, over and over. Nanabozho was running as fast as he could to get away. There was an old dead birch standing there, the inside rotted out and forming a cavity; and on seeing it, Nanabozho dove into the cavity and hid there, trembling.

"And that is what protected Nanabozho from the thunderbirds. He realized that he had done a wrong thing, and that the birch had saved him. And so he said to this birch tree, 'This is what I will do for you. You will help the people. Your bark will be used in many ways—for their homes, for their storage baskets, for their dishes. And the inside part of you, your wood, will be prized because it will provide much warmth.' And indeed, the birch has been one of the mainstays in the lives of the Ojibwa people. There is yet today a great respect for this tree."

I'm writing from the canoe, in the middle of Pocket Lake, on an evening so quiet you can hear the jaws of pine beetles as they saw through wood along the shore. I found paradise yesterday evening, a stone's throw from Lac La Croix. I'd been following a small watercourse out through the rice grass, past thousands of fragrant water lilies, each one just beginning to close its rosette of waxy, milk-colored petals against the darkness. The inky water was perfectly still, reflective again, leaving water striders to skate off from the side of the boat across a plate of clouds. At one point the flow split around a massive block of granite, and right there beavers had built dams across the entire watercourse, using the boulder as a kind of midway anchoring point. I carefully glided up to the back side of the dam and peered over, down some six feet, to where I could see the overflow tumbling across a series of smooth, rounded loaves of granite, then losing itself in the most beautiful meadow I've ever seen, blushing with wildflowers, cradled at the far edges by weaves of alder and aspen and birch. And the most remarkable sky—mare's tails and angel-hair clouds flashing pink and then coral and then rose with the fall of the sun.

Something in those few perfect moments opened a faucet inside. All day long I've been running on joy, paddling some eighteen miles and making nine portages, at various times lost in a narrow maze of marsh channels, then portaging around falls and races flashing over slabs of granite, running down the big lakes with a light breeze at my back. Before I know it, I'm just two short miles from the takeout. Darkness is coming, but still I have to almost force myself to beach at this campsite on a shelf of rock overlooking Nina Moose Lake, back in the more heavily traveled reaches of the wilderness.

Most people don't have a clue to how well sound travels across water. I can hear almost every word being said by the family on that island campsite some two hundred yards away. A sixteen-year-old is being admonished for bugging his brother and then the two of them are sent off in opposite directions to gather wood. Mom discussing whether to have green beans or pork-and-beans, and Dad grumbling about having lost the lighter. During the pre-dinner game of movie charades, I find myself better than Dad but not nearly as good as Mom or the eldest son, and later, when Mom sees a snake, I can feel the hair go up on the back of my neck at the sheer terror in her scream.

Yet all this is library whisper compared to the final arrivals of the day, a group of ten young people from a local church camp grunting up the lake in the last gray light, singing at the top of their lungs: "If you're happy and you know it, say Amen." Just offshore they give me a hearty wave and like other groups I've met, are thoroughly shocked to learn that I'm alone (to Midwesterners, people alone are either to be pitied or arrested), at which point I feel a flash of terror because I know that in thirty minutes they'll be back here, trying to drag me to the revival. In truth, though, the faithful coming back to the wilderness, which a Presbyterian preacher friend says they're doing more and more these days, is probably the best thing Christianity has done since it did it the last time, right after Joe Knowles came strutting out of the Maine wilderness. As darkness falls, I can hear the family across the lake singing (Mom has finally stopped saying how she wants to go home because of the snake), the members of the church camp next door talking low, praying for me, I suppose — me and one other chap who arrived alone by sea kayak. I lie low, happy when the rain finally comes and sends everyone to bed.

At the final portage, on a gray morning hung with the promise of rain, I meet Mary, waiting for her husband and their two daughters to arrive with the rest of the gear. We strike up a conversation. She tells me that both her grandfather and father were canoe guides, and how when she was a little girl she was constantly pestering her father to teach her the skills, but that he always said women just didn't do that sort of thing. I wonder to myself what he would have done had Kathleen Anderson been his daughter — the sled-dog musher, kayak trip leader, owner of Winter Moon. "Do you think things are different for girls today?" I ask.

"Well, a couple of years back I went on an all-women's group. We did get teased a couple of times — remarks were made. But we blew them off. Look, I'm a teacher, and I'd never be able to go back to work in the fall if I didn't have at least one week up in these woods."

I've always had more trouble than most when it comes to switching gears from the wilderness back to civilization. It's this slightly nauseating sensation of being overwhelmed by a lot of stuff — silly things like popcorn poppers and gel-filled bicycle seats; and at the stores, shelves full of cheddar pretzels and cherry Chap Stick, angled toothbrushes and fake tattoos and porcelain figurines of mermaids and beagles.

This particular coming out of the backcountry, though, ends up being easier than usual thanks to the fact that my first stop comes after a long walk from my takeout on the Little Nina Moose River down a dirt road through the woods and back to Charlie and Connie Cowden's house, where I can sit on a bench at a pinewood table and drink tea and listen to Canada warblers calling through the open windows, trade a few stories, eat beaver and blueberries and wild rice. Clearly, this is the better way.

"I remember when my folks first came up here from down south," Charlie is saying. "Hell, I was living in a tiny cabin with an old privy out back, and Mom was scared to use it because of the bears and the wolves and anything else that moved. I always assumed they thought I was goofy, because the truth is, a lot of people did. But then in snatches of conversation, other people would tell me that Dad was bragging about his kid being up here in the woods living like a brush ape, going on and on about it, I guess experiencing an old dream of his own through me, maybe even wishing he'd have done the same."

Charlie and Connie say that if you find a partner who'll stick it out with you for six months in this kind of life, as a couple you've got a chance. Charlie and his first wife, whom he met while he was guiding, never made it. "For her, it was a matter of leaving a place where she had material things—the car, the electricity, the sewing machine, and backing up fifty years. Taking a step backward when everyone else she knew was going forward. A lot of it was peer pressure, friends telling her she was nuts to be living like she was, with a little baby in a one-room cabin with no electricity and no running water. You know, I've been trapping ever since I was a teenager, and my goal was always to run the trap lines by dog team in some remote area where the snow was four feet deep. Really, this place was supposed to be just a stop on my way to Alaska. By the time I was seventeen I'd read every book on the subject I could get my hands on.

That was the dream that drove me. But it's not for everyone. It sure wasn't for her."

By the time I walk out the door and down the steps, Charlie and Connie have loaded me with a Sigurd Olson book I somehow missed reading, two quarts of blueberries, and at least a pound of wild rice, all collected by hand, and this too makes it just a little bit easier to think of heading west, out of the woods and across a thousand miles of plains, toward home.

Chapter Eleven

The leaving begins near Mahnomen, Minnesota, on the White Earth Indian Reservation, in a land tossed with a thousand ponds and kettle holes and flat, silent streams lined with strips of cattails. And between all that, long-reaching fields of sunflowers standing at attention, every plate-sized bloom turned back the way I came, facing into the rising sun. The trees don't go all at once, of course. They scatter by degrees, pulling farther and farther back from the old concrete highway until by the town of Ada, on the Wild Rice River, the best of them are little more than green smudges in the rearview mirror. Out here on the prairie, uncrowded by woods, the small towns are trying to act like big ones, sprawling in every direction, squatting beside Main Streets big enough to funnel a decent rush hour and a good-sized marching band.

Sitting beside me on the passenger seat is a birch basket given to me by Amelia Legarde, the Ojibwa storyteller, placed in my hands right as I was walking out the door of her house in Duluth. "This is for you," was all she said. "I want you to have it." It wasn't made by weaving, the way we usually think of baskets, but rather from a single piece of bark fourteen inches tall and three feet wide, wrapped into a cylinder and then closed at the seam with strips of basswood. The top and bottom edges are trimmed with scalloped strips of winter bark, rust-red, with thin, ivory-colored blisters. Sort of like a log drum with no top. Looking at it reminds me of how in some cultures during certain rites of passage, an empty chalice was placed in a prominent location—one of those archetypal symbols meant to remind people of the empty space that lies between who they were and who they'll be. A way of nudging them into being on the lookout for new beginnings.

It's a strange time to be coming into North Dakota. Last night, Michael Moore's program *TV Nation* made big fun of the state, going for that whole icebox thing—the howling blizzards and the empty airports, how it's the least-visited state in America. Today everyone is talking about it: old farmers in Portland, the gas-station attendant, the waitress in Mayville, members of the congregation from the Bruflat Lutheran Church. The Department of Tourism director and the governor are on the radio, sounding very sincere, telling everyone how they tried to show Moore the highlights of the state, all to no avail. I say forget it. In fact, I'm not so sure they shouldn't be thankful. If I were a North Dakotan I'd probably be on my knees giving thanks for these clean skies and kettle holes full of ducks, and blissful, quiet highways, even if they are drifted over half the year with snow.

I like this state. It's the kind of sprawling, windblasted place that builds humble, hopeful people—a whack on the side of the head for those lost in the cerebral, the brace on the back that helps straighten the spine. Besides, I've always had the most pleasant mental rambles while driving across North Dakota, as if the whole state was like that porch the woman who owned the lodge in Maine talked about, the one where she keeps trying to make her guests just sit for an hour and stop being distracted, get to know themselves again. Relax. This is even better because you don't have any choice. Nobody has to be here coaching you to be in the moment, because early on, the land drives you right down into surrender. Only a fool would fight against North Dakota.

West from Carrington it's a sweet, lonely float across the golden rills of the prairie, under a platter of blue sky so big you can be looking straight down and still feel it. It's less like driving than riding in a railroad club car, which may explain why two of the six drivers who passed me going in the other direction over the last thirty miles were reading newspapers. Swap shows are the local programming option of choice on AM radio—electronic garage sales. People are calling in to sell everything from dalmatians to trash compactors to tractor tires (weather-checked and on the rim), looking to buy woodstoves and trailer hitches and babysitters.

Ever so slowly the land is changing, increasingly cut by twisted coulees, agriculture turning from corn and beans to dry land crops and cattle. Haystacks are coming farther and farther apart now, the hay less likely to be baled than rolled into great rounded humps that from a distance look like nothing so much as giant pieces of shredded wheat. Modest trees stand beside the houses, doing their best to hang on, and here and there cottonwood groves can be seen huddling in ditch pockets and at the bottoms of the larger coulees. Old Aeromotor windmills roll by, some with their blades torn off by the winds. The air gets clearer, more pungent-smelling, like the West.

As I've said, I always end up doing a lot of thinking while driving across the open sprawls of this state, and today is no exception. Mostly I keep going back to the people I've left behind in the woods: Barry and Lori Dana, Garrett and Alexandra Conover, Lester Simpson and Henry Johnson and Amelia Legarde, Deb Sylvester and Charlie Cowden. It's while lost in this reverie, rolling through a yawning patch of prairie the color of cornhusks, just west of Mercer and south of the turtle races at Turtle Lake, in a place where you can't buy a tree, it suddenly hits me. What pushed the woods to the outside edges of my life eight years ago wasn't that I lost my appreciation for them, but only that I stopped *practicing* them. I was fighting so hard, struggling like so many others against the careless polluting of rivers, the carving up of winter range, the plans for gold mines in high country that can never be reclaimed. Important battles, all of them. But it got to the point where there was nothing left but the fighting. I lost the mundane. I became less a lover to the woods than a bodyguard. No matter how my head might be exploding with good intentions toward the earth, unless my brand of nature advocacy is rooted in something palpable, concrete, common as dirt, I will always end up burned out in bad religion. It's Garrett Conover's decision to link himself to his surroundings with a draw knife and a canvas canoe, to wear wool sweaters in the rain. It's Darla Simpson drinking half-gallons of catnip tea to beat a cold, or Charlie Cowden harvesting rice. It's the relationship, stupid.

I should have made the connection way back on the Hudson River, at Olana, home of that great American landscape painter Frederick Church. I remember the curator saying how Church was depressed almost beyond function when in the latter 1800s the country began turning away from nature art and poetry, away from those precious sermons in the stones. He should've walked out of that fancy mansion of his, wandered down the hill and grabbed a couple of those oak saplings he kept the gardeners busy sticking in the ground, made it his new mission to scoop out a few holes in the earth with his bare hands and see if he could make one of them grow.

Several years ago I heard this amazing story, told to me

by a guy in his mid-sixties, a dear friend of mine, extremely well-educated and the most gifted, meticulous naturalist I've ever known. He grew up poor during the Depression on a farm back in one of the woodland states, hunting deer and squirrels, even making his own arrows, roaming the forests with something close to fever. One day we were having a quiet conversation at his home when he got up and shut the door to the room, came back and sat down, leaned forward in his chair and looked me right in the eye, said he was about to tell me something he'd never told anyone before. That he wanted to share this thing that happened to him fifty years earlier, but that he still thought about almost every day of his life.

"I was fifteen," he said. "Still living with my folks on the farm. It was real late on a summer night, that time right in the middle from dusk to dawn—warm, with a full moon shining through my bedroom window. I'm not sure how to tell this . . . I mean, it felt like a dream, sounds like one. But it wasn't. I'm laying there and all of a sudden I'm just overcome by this urge to head into the pasture. I crawl out of bed and go outside—buck-naked, mind you—and before I knew it, I was running through those fields, weaving along the edge of the woods. No, running's not right. I was *leaping*, like a damned deer! Almost floating. It went on and on—I don't know for how long, maybe a half-hour—running in lines and big circles, racing around barefoot without ever feeling tired. It was like the whole night—the moon and grass and deer and bugs—was in my blood, pumping through my veins, letting me do all manner of amazing things I'd never done before. And never since."

And then he stopped talking, and his eyes narrowed back to normal, he shook his head and gazed around the room, like somebody coming out of a trance.

Whatever that epiphany was—a waking dream, or the gods coming down for a fast dance in the body of a country boy—I think it could have happened only to someone like him, someone who *practiced* the woods. A person for whom nature wasn't mistress, but wife. Someone who knew the smell of bark and dry earth, who was likely as not to clock hours by the roll of shadows and the months by their blooms, someone who'd stumbled and fallen and left his blood lying on the rocks.

"Like I say," he told me, "nothing like it ever happened again. But then, one time is enough to change you. It's not that I lived any different afterward. I just thought better of it. There was more life to hold on to."

"Chop wood and carry water," the teacher tells the student. "And perhaps enlightenment will come."

"And after enlightenment?" the student asks.

"Chop wood and carry water."

By the time my head floats back to the road, it's past time for a break. And what better place than the tiny village of Zap, North Dakota—"A Little Town with a Big Heart," as the welcome sign says? It was in Zap that in 1969 there occurred one of the most outrageous events in an otherwise fairly quiet twentieth century. A journalism student by the name of Kevin Carvell, bitten by spring fever but too poor to make the expedition south to warmer climates, decided to invite some of his fellow college students to snub the rush to Florida, the Gulf Coast, the Bahamas. Surely, he wrote in *The Spectrum*, North Dakota State's college newspaper, there must be an equivalent to Fort Lauderdale right here in the far north.

"We began to search and found the perfect spot, a truly idyllic setting, a Garden of Paradise, unspoiled and just asking for carefree students to rescue it from its oblivion." It was a town of two hundred fifty in the western part of the state—one café, one grocery store, a lumberyard, two bars, and two gas stations. It was Zap. Carvell went on to promise those who arrived on Friday, May 9, such exciting adventures as watching school get out, eating Zap burgers at the Zap Café, slipping coins into the jukebox and listening to the "Heartbreak Waltz" and the "Swinging Benny Polka." On Saturday there was to be an "honest-to-God rock dance," featuring the Outcasts from Minot, as well as "a full program of orgies, brawls, freakouts and arrests."

It was the last story Kevin Carvell would ever write as editor for *The Spectrum*. How could he have known that the Associated Press would pick up the piece, that his little party would end up being announced on all three network news broadcasts, *The Today Show*, in *The Los Angeles Times*, and *The Denver Post*? The zip to Zap was underway. Yet even with all this somewhat alarming publicity, the good mayor of Zap, Norman Fuchs, put on his best smile and prepared to welcome the crowds of young fun-seekers. After all, how bad could it be? He even sent a letter through *The Spectrum* welcoming the North Dakota State students, listing the special treats being planned for them. There would be "barbecued beef, styled à la chow line, fleisch kuechle with cow-belle sauce (a kind of meat pie), hot dogs with or without bun, the Outcasts for your rhythm release, an ocean full of suds, plenty of rooms for the action, and Zip-Zap souvenirs."

While the official kickoff was scheduled for Saturday night, a lot of people got there on Friday. Two thousand of them, with more on the way, some traveling from as far away as Florida. By that evening there were an awful lot of drunk people shivering in the cold out on Main Street, and some of them decided to build an enormous bonfire, using wood from a nearby building. When the volunteer fire department arrived, some of the kids thought to take the hose into Lucky's Bar—to wash the place out a little, they said, which some swear was a reaction to the guys who'd leased Lucky's suddenly deciding to raise the price of beer to fifty cents a can. Another bar, the Lignite, was completely trashed later that night. In the end, the police threw up their hands—some even joined the party—and the fire truck drove away and let the bonfire burn.

By dawn on Saturday, the good citizens of Zap had had enough, and the mayor placed a call to the National Guard. It was just after six o'clock in the morning on May 10 when Norman Fuchs walked out in front of a line of guardsmen with rifles and bayonets and officially retracted his welcome. The students, almost three thousand strong now, scattered across the bleak countryside into neighboring small towns and were eventually chased by State Police and the National Guard all the way to Bismarck. A few, though, managed to find silver linings. Sandy Huseby, for one, who also served a stint as editor of *The Spectrum,* went to Washington shortly after the fiasco, said she funded her trip and an entire month of living expenses just by selling Zip-to-Zap T-shirts. "Who knows?" she mused. "This might have been the inspiration for Woodstock."

Today, Zap is decidedly calmer. In fact, there's only one person visible when I arrive, an elderly woman crossing the street on her way to the post office. There's a tiny market, a hair salon, the Lignite and Shooters bars, one church, and the Union State Bank, which is housed in a trailer. The coal mine in Beulah closed down two years ago, and that, I'm told, has made this quiet town even quieter than before.

I sit on a stool at a cherry-colored bar in the Lignite with Carol, the bartender (the booths that were trashed in 1969 have never been replaced). I'm the only customer. I sip at a can of Bud; Carol flips her dark hair away from her glasses, settles behind the bar on a high chair, tells me she's going into the hospital in a couple of weeks so the doctors can treat her anemia, an event she says she's really looking forward to so she can finally get some rest, what with farming full-time in addition to this bartending job. I find out that she was one of those at the original Zip-to-Zap, which of course forces me to order another beer and ask her what it was like.

"Well," she says, lighting up a fresh cigarette, wincing a little, "people were just fornicating everywhere you looked. Every side street, every corner. Other stuff, too. Disgusting. I remember one guy sitting on top of the dance hall—right here next to the bar—taking a crap down onto the street below. The stoops right out here were a foot deep in beer cans."

Remarkably, despite all that disgusting stuff, the little town of Zap doesn't exactly seem eager to forget. The walls of the trailer that houses the Union State Bank also serve as repository for all things having to do with the event, and when I go over there later, I'm amazed to find them covered with newspaper stories. Included in the collection are articles from a 1989 twenty-year "community remembrance" of the Zap-in, which featured a dance, barbecue, and ceremony, all meant to show appreciation to the original attendees for putting Zap on the map. And then there was the twenty-fifth anniversary party, held this past May. Evidently nobody wanted to spend tax dollars on police for the thing, but all in all it came off great—some three thousand people, and everyone well-behaved. Zip-to-Zap even has a full page dedicated to it in the town's Diamond Jubilee historical book, published in 1988, a copy of which I buy from Carol the bartender for twelve dollars. Back out in the van, I open it and on the very first page this is what it says: "We wish to welcome everyone to Zap and hope that through our efforts to give you the best entertainment, you will have a pleasant time and a lifelong memory."

And Michael Moore says there's nothing to do in North Dakota.

Chapter Twelve

The old Chevy van is empty again. Free of backpacks and canoe paddles, life jacket and river sandals and moonshine, buckeyes and pennyroyal and boxes of books, cameras and maps and field guides, rice and blueberries from Charlie and Connie, grape jam and beets and butter beans from Pearl. There are thirty hours of taped conversations stacked on my desk, along with two spirals full of notes, the pages on one warped and the ink smudged by the Minnesota rain. The birch-bark basket from Amelia Legarde is sitting in my living room next to the rocking chair, half-filled with pinecones of ponderosa and spruce and whitebark, keepsakes from other journeys, other woods.

You'd think it might be a big deal for me to be in my own bed again, but two nights after I got back I parked the van in the woods beside the house and slept there instead. I've been home for almost a month now, and there are still mornings when I wake up at dawn and have to think over where I am, catch myself trying to figure out what forest I'll be wandering through today. But it's the home woods that matter now: this loose weave of aspen and cottonwood falling from the toes of the Beartooth Mountains, down the granite belly of the valley, past every door and window of our house and on north through town, thinning out, in the end able to claim only the creek banks, clinging to them all the way to the Yellowstone.

Of course it's nowhere near as diverse as the forests of Tennessee. Not even close. The autumn colors pale in comparison to the riotous shows in New England, and anyone searching for the perfect load of cabinet logs, or even for firewood, would take one look and keep on going. Yet this is the forest that carries the seasons that measure my life. These are the trees that play the songs I know best.

When Jane and I first started living in this house six years ago I spent a lot of time upstairs, looking south out of the second-story windows toward the distant mountains. These days I seem to be more of a downstairs sort, content to peer out the kitchen windows and watch chickadees feeding in the cottonwoods, dippers plunging into stream eddies, fishing for insects. Now that fall's here we lie in bed at night and wait for a certain neighbor of ours, a black bear named Spot, who likes to clomp across the deck and look in the sliding door of our bedroom. Jane says he's trying to get me to put the bird feeder back up, the one he smashes to pieces at every chance for a few lousy bites of sunflower seed. And if not Spot, then moose out there tugging on the branches of young aspen, whitetails tearing at clover, the occasional raccoon.

I've been trying to keep my head in the dirt. On Saturday mornings a friend stops by and we drive his pickup into the Pryor Mountains and spend the day cutting firewood, sit on the tailgate in late afternoon, full of sawdust, sharpening the chains on the saws, trying to figure how much more we need until we have enough. And once in a while I drive over to

Absarokee, to a willow-framed sweat lodge a guy built on a bank of the West Rosebud River, crawl in for three or four rounds of good heat, break each one with a bucket of cold water poured over my head. I fish with my friends who love to fish, and give more thanks for the ones we catch and eat than I used to. Now and then I pluck a couple of rose hips and dry a little yarrow for tea, quit the office early and walk down to the creek just to count the number of trees the beaver have cut down. I watch elk massing on the refuge outside of town and wonder how they'll fare in the coming winter, stand outside on the porch in the last light of evening and wait for a glimpse of southbound Canada geese, feeling even now how fine it will be to have them dropping back again out of the blustery skies of spring.

The myths of long ago speak of a powerful courage to change that can ignite in anyone who leaves the familiar and enters the woods, either by accident or by design. That was the whole point of the original, pre-moralized versions of Red Riding Hood and Snow White, not to mention the hundreds of hero tales from Britain and Germany and ancient Greece. These characters went into the forest because it was impossible to become who they were meant to be without first going someplace where they could become utterly lost. Cut loose for a time from who they were and where they came from. Drifting clueless, facing both the beauty and the fear that awaits at the heart of every life transition, be it adolescence or marriage, divorce or sickness or old age. Were we to have forests sprawling across this country completely unused for anything other than to remind us of that, we would have a lot.

For those who drift into the trees hoping for something beyond aesthetic beauty, there seems to be a catch. A paradox. It has to do with the fact that the only way to engender deep kinship to place is to stop struggling for it, to stop always seeking insight and be content to busy yourself in ways that insight might one day find you. Maybe this year, maybe next. Out there, bent over with your kindling box in hand, scooping up branches; out there, walking by the river with your fishing pole or raspberry bucket, kneeling in the meadow with your flower press.

Out there, practicing the woods.